S A C R E D
P A U S E S

"April Yamasaki's stories and practical advice not only show us how—they make us want to pursue spiritual practices."
—*Gordon Houser, author of* Present Tense

"The world of spiritual practices can sometimes seem removed from ordinary life—as though spirituality is a luxury for those with plenty of time on their hands. April Yamasaki challenges that notion."
—*Marlene Kropf, retired denominational minister of worship, Mennonite Church USA*

"Rooted in Scripture and drawing from a rich breadth of other sources both historical and contemporary, *Sacred Pauses* offers a feast of insight with wisdom, honesty, humility, and thoughtful clarity."
—*Barbara Nickel, poet and children's author*

"This is the first spiritual disciplines book that I have read that includes the practice of 'having fun.'"
—*Marva J. Dawn, author of* Keeping the Sabbath Wholly *and* Being Well When We're Ill

"I love Yamasaki's personal, real-life stories, which draw me into her exploration of ways to draw close to God."
—*Christine Sine, executive director of Mustard Seed Associates and author of* Return to Our Senses

SACRED PAUSES

Spiritual Practices for Personal Renewal

April Yamasaki

Herald Press

Waterloo, Ontario
Harrisonburg, Virginia

Library and Archives Canada Cataloguing in Publication
Yamasaki, April
      Sacred pauses : spiritual practices for personal
renewal / April Yamasaki.
   ISBN 978-0-8361-9685-6
      1. Christian life. I. Title.
BV4501.3.Y34 2013   248   C2012-907148-X

Unless otherwise noted, Scripture text is quoted, with permission, from the *New Revised Standard Version*, © 1989, Division of Christian Education of the National Council of Churches of Christ in the United States of America.

SACRED PAUSES
Copyright © 2013 by April Yamasaki
      Published in Canada by Herald Press, Waterloo, Ontario N2L 6H7.
      Released simultaneously in the United States of America by
      Herald Press, Harrisonburg, Virginia 22802. All rights reserved.
Library of Congress Control Number: 2012951901
Canadian Entry Number: C2012-907148-X
International Standard Book Number: 978-0-8361-9685-6
Printed in United States of America
Cover design by Reuben Graham, design by Joshua Byler
Cover photo by Zheng Long/iStockphoto/Thinkstock

To order or request information, please call 1-800-245-7894 in the U.S. or 1-800-631-6535 in Canada. Or visit www.heraldpress.com.

18 17 16 15 14 13   10 9 8 7 6 5 4 3 2

For all those seeking rest and personal renewal

Table of Contents

Foreword

Not so long ago, "Fine" was usually the answer to the question "How are you?" Nowadays, more and more often, I hear people respond, "Busy." (One friend puts this a little more subtly: "Still standing.") This change is significant.

In my last pastorate, during a period of congregational discernment, our members concluded that a primary faith challenge they faced was busyness. The elders agreed to address this issue but delayed several years before doing so—they had too much to do! I realized then that busyness is a *pastoral* concern.

I once walked eight hundred kilometers (five hundred miles) on the Camino de Santiago, a pilgrimage route in Spain that tens of thousands of people walk every year. While this path is Christian in origin, most who register for it do not identify themselves as Christian. Many pilgrims I encountered told me they were "not religious" or "spiritual but not religious." But—get this—almost all of them talked to me about their deep dissatisfaction with the quality and pace of their lives. I realized that busyness is an *evangelistic* and *missional* concern.

In fact, we are busier than ever before. This is not a hypothetical or nostalgic claim. We work longer hours. "Labor-saving" devices increase demands on us. We are tethered 24/7 to technologically expedited expectations. These realities drive our culture's interest in spirituality.

But what happens when Christians live the same disconnected, disoriented ways as everyone else? Some Christians give up: "We have no choice"; "It is what it is." I notice that I no longer hear as much "quiet time" or "daily devotions" terminology. Perhaps fewer Christians are taking up these practices. I once read a fine and inspiring book on the Sabbath but was disheartened when the author declared that it is no longer possible for Christians to observe this priority as a day set apart. If Sabbath is a divinely provided gift, surely not even our culture—obsessed as it is with productivity, consumerism, technology—need overwhelm us.

Other Christians double down on legalistic rules and requirements. They suggest programs of three or four or seven points of action over a certain number of days or weeks. But I worry about such approaches, too. They feel onerous, and they add to busyness. Besides, surely Christian formation is something more than outcomes-oriented, step-by-step, time-limited techniques. Jesus said that the wind of the Spirit blows in ways beyond our control, understanding, or manipulation. Spiritual formation is not about mastery.

So where do we turn?

I am excited by April Yamasaki's new book. She is a writer and pastor I have admired for years, long showing her devotion to congregational life, spiritual growth and formation, and scriptural engagement. And she always does this through carefully crafted writing. Her lifetime of reflection on such matters culminates with this book, where she tackles precisely the kinds of concerns that are so pressing for us now in our culture. She wonders: "What would it take to feel renewed every day? . . . What if we could take time out every day? Live a renewed life every day? Be refreshed by God every day?"

To that end, she proposes experimenting with modest *practices*—choosing everyday icons of refreshment, slowing down and journaling, savoring silence, pondering Scriptures, walking prayerfully, exploring solitude, celebrating fun, and many more.

Yamasaki shows that many spiritual practices are within reach. Small but modest, their effect on us can be cumulative. View a Scripture passage from a new angle. Enjoy scenery as you stroll in your neighborhood. Take a new look at an old familiar prayer.

The issue with spiritual practices is never perfection, she reveals, but rather persistence in pursuing opportunities to engage God and dwell in the abundant life God longs for us to know. Just try them, she encourages us; you might like them. There is a reason that they have been important to so many believers who have gone before us.

She nudges us to practice some unfamiliar approaches and to be open to finding something unexpectedly enjoyable.

All this she does with a gentle, invitational spirit, one that is informed by long-standing Christian spiritual formation traditions. She illustrates her teaching with humble and homey testimonies rooted in real life as a minister, daughter, and spouse. I envy those who have Yamasaki as their pastor, but this book widens her ministry; she now becomes a wise spiritual director to many readers.

The spiritual life is not complicated and neither are many spiritual practices. Most such disciplines are simple, straight-forward, and commonsensical. All that they require is some consistency and regularity. The sacred pauses that Yamasaki explores and recommends are rewarding in and of themselves, but they have the potential to transform the whole of our lives.

Yes, life is full and challenging. But Yamasaki invites us to "take a load off" and rest in God's grace. Live out the wisdom of this book and the next time someone asks how you are, you may well be tempted to respond, "Still thriving."

—*Arthur Boers, author of* Living into Focus: Choosing What Matters in an Age of Distractions

Introduction

A few years ago, my husband and I were driving home after a brief vacation in Oregon. The previous month had been difficult, with the death of a dear church member followed by the death of my father-in-law. Life had been intense both pastorally and personally, so I had been looking forward to a time of rest and re-creation.

Those few days turned out to be just what I needed. I went to bed early and slept late, took long walks, wrote in my journal, and generally let go of feeling responsible for everything. On the drive home, I was much more relaxed as we stopped for ice cream and browsed in one of my favorite bookstores.

On the sale rack, I saw *28 Days to a New You* and then *The 30-Day Total Health Makeover*. I didn't buy either of them, but those two books started me thinking.

What would it take to feel renewed every day? Instead of waiting for a vacation to smooth out the knots of tension from everyday life, instead of waiting until the end of the week to shed our weariness, what if we could take time out every day? Live a renewed life every day? Be refreshed by God every day?

That's when I began to think about spiritual disciplines in a new way. I already loved my early morning quiet times—the silence before the rest of the world was awake, lighting a candle, writing in my journal, reading Scripture, praying. But what if I could weave these and other spiritual practices into the rest of my day as times of personal renewal?

I didn't have the words for it then, but now I know that I was longing for the sacred pause in my morning quiet times. I wanted more sacred pauses in the middle of the day—anywhere and at any time—to refresh and renew my spirit, to keep me grounded and sustained by God's Spirit.

That longing has become this book.

Sacred Pauses is for those who are looking for something more. For the busy professional caught up in paperwork and meetings, for the construction worker framing a house, for the young mother at home, for the student wondering about next steps, for those who are

> Spiritual discipline, spiritual practice, spiritual exercise. These phrases are often used interchangeably, but, for the most part, I focus on spiritual *practice*—not primarily for correcting something wrong, not with the expectation that I will do it perfectly according to some objective standard, but as something I am learning to do, and that anyone can do.

retired or just plain tired. There is more to life than the things that occupy our immediate attention. We can pause, connect more deeply with ourselves and with God, and be renewed.

To that end, this book is designed to be personal, practical, flexible, and used in whatever way works best for you. From "Creating Space" to "Ending Well," each chapter highlights a spiritual exercise that is grounded in Scripture, illustrated with personal examples, and meant to be put into practice in the midst of daily life. "Creating Space," "Praying Scripture," and other practices are not simply stories about other people. These are sacred pauses that you can try for yourself.

Sometimes a chapter will offer just one main idea that you can take in a variety of directions—like choosing an everyday icon in chapter 1. At other times, as in chapter 6, you'll have several options—like going for a nature walk or a prayer walk around your neighborhood, or taking a longer hike. You might not try everything, but trying something from each chapter is a good way to explore what's refreshing to you and what's not; what you immediately resonate with, and what might take more practice.

Reading Scripture, praying, fasting, and other classic disciplines have a long history in the Christian tradition. Valuing relationships, making music, and some of the other practices in this book have not generally been recognized in the same way. But all of these share a common thread in their capacity for refreshment and personal renewal as we allow God to work in us.

Entire books have been written on any one of these practices, so the intention here is not to be comprehensive, but to provide an introduction, give opportunity for practical exploration, and kindle a desire for more.

Feel free to use this book in any way that works for you. Try it as a daily personal retreat, reading one chapter a day, six days a week, for three weeks. Or scale back, and read through the book more slowly, section by section. If you skip a day or a week or a spiritual practice, don't berate yourself for a lack of discipline or spend time feeling guilty. Instead, simply pick up where you left off, or give yourself permission to skip that part or combine it with the next.

Although these spiritual practices are meant to build on one another, you can choose to ignore the order entirely and begin with the spiritual practice or theme that speaks most strongly to you. Use this book on your own, in tandem with a friend or small group, or even as a congregation. The choice is yours, and you can't do it wrong.

Sacred pauses remind us that our lives are in God's hands. As the psalmist writes during a difficult time in his own life, "But I trust in you, O LORD; I say, 'You are my God.' My times are in your hand."[1] We can be assured of God's presence and care at all times—when we need time out, when we take time out, at any time.

---

1. Psalm 31:14-15a.

In that spirit of hope and confidence in God, I offer you this blessing for all your sacred pauses: "Now may the Lord of peace himself give you peace at all times in all ways. The Lord be with all of you."[2]

—*April Yamasaki*

---

2. 2 Thessalonians 3:16.

1

Creating Space

_____

The LORD is my shepherd, I shall not want.
He makes me lie down in green pastures;
he leads me beside still waters;
he restores my soul.
Psalm 23:1-3a

On my desk at home, I keep a small tray with a matching coaster and china coffee mug given to me one Christmas by one of my sisters. Each piece is delicately painted with pictures of various herbs and their flowers. The familiar rosemary and sage remind me of the herbs that I grow in my own garden, and the less familiar borage and tansy remind me that there are always new things to explore. No matter how cluttered my desk gets with piles of books, assorted file folders, and notes to myself, I always reserve a spot for my special tray, with the mug on its coaster and space alongside for a morning muffin or afternoon cookie. That simple coffee set has become a favorite of mine—a thoughtful gift, chosen with care, that always has a place of honor on my desk.

One time after we had overnight house guests, I noticed that someone had used my special china mug for an early morning coffee. It must have seemed quite natural to use it, since it was clean and close at hand on my desk right beside the kitchen. I didn't mind at all—I'm glad when house guests make themselves at home—but that discovery made me smile because I've never actually used that mug for coffee, tea, water, or anything else. And although there's room on the tray for a sweet treat of some kind, I've never used it for that either.

What my house guests hadn't realized is that my favorite coffee set is not about coffee at all. Instead, it serves as my reminder of sacred pause. In the early morning as I spend some quiet time alone, it makes my desk more a place of personal refreshment than a place of work. In the middle of a busy day as I pass by my desk, the coffee set reminds me that God is with me. I can breathe a prayer as I go past. I can pause between the fourth and fifth ring of the telephone and give thanks to God the great Shepherd, who gives me rest and leads me and restores my soul. In this way, my coffee set is well used—as a reminder to pause for refreshment and renewal even in the midst of daily life.

Retreat

The word *retreat* means to move back, and a spiritual retreat most often involves a physical withdrawal, leaving the normal surroundings of home, work, and family, and withdrawing for a time to a mountain retreat center, a cabin in the woods, a lakeside camp, or other quiet place. Away from the responsibilities of daily life; away from traffic, telephone, television, Internet, and other distractions; time on retreat may be spent alone or in community, with a spiritual director or as a group.

Time may be given over largely to prayer and reflection; reading Scripture and seeking God; solitude and silence; spiritual direction and finding a new sense of purpose; slowing down and becoming more centered. On a group retreat, there is opportunity for corporate worship and study, reenvisioning and planning together, connecting with others, and making new friends. Many retreat settings offer fresh air, natural surroundings, pleasant places to walk, and good food. A retreat to "get away from it all" lends itself to rest and renewal, reconnecting with yourself and with God, finding new clarity and personal transformation.

In the Bible, Jesus spends time on retreat in the wilderness for what the gospel of Matthew describes as "forty days and forty nights," recalling the people of Israel who spent forty years in the wilderness before they finally reached the Promised Land, and recalling Moses fasting "forty days and forty nights" before he received the two stone tablets of the covenant. Like the new Israel and the new Moses, Jesus does not retreat for rest and relaxation. Instead, his retreat is an intense period of solitude and fasting, a time for testing his call from God, a time for struggling with temptation, a time for applying Scripture to the challenges that he faced. For Jesus, rest and renewal comes only at the end of his retreat, when "the devil left him, and suddenly angels came and waited on him."[1]

The prophet Elijah travels "forty days and forty nights" on a personal retreat of sorts to Mount Horeb. Uncompromising and outspoken, Elijah had gotten himself in trouble with King Ahab and his wife, Jezebel, who had threatened to have the prophet killed. So Elijah runs into the wilderness as far as he can go—on a retreat that is part genuine soul-searching and part escape for his life, and along the way, he encounters God in new ways and finds new purpose for his life and ministry.[2]

The apostle Paul has a similar experience. The chronology is not entirely clear, but from the brief retelling of his story in one of his letters, it is soon after his encounter with the risen Christ that Paul retreats for a time to Arabia—not out of fear for his life, but perhaps to reflect on his earlier zeal to persecute the followers of Jesus and what that now means in light of his newfound faith. Like Elijah, he apparently encounters God in a new way and finds a new purpose, for after some time away, he returns to Damascus where he begins to proclaim Jesus. Still a man of passion, the former persecutor is transformed into a preacher and fervent church planter.[3]

---

1. Matthew 4:1-11; cf. Deuteronomy 8:2; 9:9-11.
2. 1 Kings 19.
3. Galatians 1:13-17; Acts 9:19b-22.

In the Bible, such soul-searching is not limited to times of retreat in remote areas. Silence, solitude, searching the Scriptures, encountering God in prayer, new clarity of purpose, personal transformation all take place in many other contexts. In the Sermon on the Mount, Jesus tells his followers, "[W]henever you pray, go into your room and shut the door."[4] He himself would spend time in prayer at critical points in his ministry—early in the morning before beginning his public ministry of preaching and healing throughout Galilee,[5] when he speaks to his disciples about his coming suffering,[6] even on the night of his arrest.[7] The psalmist retreats to his bed for silence, confession, meditation, and prayer.[8] The weekly Sabbath and other religious festivals throughout the year serve as regular opportunities for worship, prayer, and reading of Scripture.[9]

> In Scripture, the weekly Sabbath was given as a time of rest and worship. A sacred pause in the middle of a day is like a mini-retreat or a mini-Sabbath.

In periods of extended retreat and in more ordinary times woven into daily life, the critical issue is not geography. A room at home may serve just as well for prayer as the wilderness—for God is at work in the wilderness, on the mountain top, at home, and everywhere. God is our place of refuge and renewal,[10] the God who is at work in us,[11] the One in whom "we live and move and have our being."[12]

Spiritually speaking, a retreat is really less about physical space and more about personal focus and being deliberately

4. Matthew 6:6.
5. Mark 1:35.
6. John 17:1-26.
7. Luke 22:39-46.
8. Psalms 4:4; 63:6.
9. Exodus 20:8-11; 23:12; 34:21-24.
10. Psalms 31:1-2; 46:1; 51:10-12; 71:1-3.
11. Philippians 2:13.
12. Acts 17:28.

attentive to God; less about seeing the wilderness and more about how we see ourselves; less about traveling to somewhere else and more about placing ourselves before God. That's what makes it possible to retreat anywhere and anytime, even without packing a suitcase and leaving home.

To be sure, there are unique challenges to retreating at home. It may be more difficult to hear God's voice in the midst of all the other clamoring voices in our world and even within our own families and households. It may be more difficult to slow down if we remain immersed in our instant-on, do-it-now, hurry-up culture. At home with spouse and children or roommates close at hand, we may find it harder to close the door for prayer than if we actually went away. How can we turn off our busy spirit that's so easily distracted by a stack of work brought home from school or office, the beep of another text message, the thought of a counter full of dishes waiting to be washed, or the lure of whatever ballgame happens to be on television?

One of the classic models for retreat is *The Spiritual Exercises of St. Ignatius of Loyola,* **which is organized into four weeks to be completed along with a spiritual director. But even Saint Ignatius seemed to realize that was not possible or practical for everyone. In his opening instructions, he included a "Nineteenth Annotation" that allowed for a part-time retreat at home.**

Is it possible to incorporate spiritual practice into daily life? Can we weave spiritual practice into our lives so it's not just about the time we can set apart but about our entire day? After all, wherever we may be, however busy or distracted or restless, however much or little time we can set aside, Scripture assures us that God is ever present. What the psalmist says is true for us as well:

> Where can I go from your spirit?
> Or where can I flee from your presence?
> If I ascend to heaven, you are there;
> if I make my bed in Sheol, you are there.

If I take the wings of the morning
and settle at the farthest limits of the sea,
even there your hand shall lead me,
and your right hand shall hold me fast.[13]

In the New Testament, Jesus is given the name Emmanuel, which means "God is with us,"[14] and he tells his followers, "Remember, I am with you always, to the end of the age."[15]

God's presence around us, behind us, before us, everywhere, makes possible the testimony of Brother Lawrence in *The Practice of the Presence of God*: "The time of business," said he, "does not with me differ from the time of prayer; and in the noise and clutter of my kitchen, while several persons are at the same time calling for different things, I possess God in as great tranquillity as if I were upon my knees at the Blessed Sacrament."[16]

Spiritual practice is one way of recognizing that God is always with us, and there is room in our ordinary lives to be with God. Scripture, prayer, paying attention, and other practices can be sacred pauses—for a greater awareness of God and deeper personal growth, for more healthy and holy living.

Sacred pause: choose an everyday icon

A number of years ago, when a friend returned from a trip to Ukraine, she brought back an icon as a gift to celebrate my ordination. Within the wooden frame is a picture of Jesus, a look of solemn compassion on his face, his hand raised in a gesture of forgiveness and blessing. It's a work of art, but as an icon it is more than that; it's meant also as a symbol, to point beyond itself to something more. In this case, the icon

---

13. Psalm 139:7-10.
14. Matthew 1:23.
15. Matthew 28:20.
16. Brother Lawrence, *The Practice of the Presence of God: The Best Rule of Holy Life*, date unknown, http://www.ccel.org/ccel/lawrence/practice.pdf, 13.

is a symbol of Jesus' ongoing presence and mercy, a symbol of God's blessing on my ordination to pastoral ministry, a symbol of support and friendship.

An icon is generally a piece of religious art like this picture of Jesus that I keep in my church office. But the coffee set on my desk at home is a kind of everyday icon. Much more than a coffee set, it has become a symbol that points beyond itself to something more. As it sits on my desk, it's an everyday icon that points to spiritual practice and personal renewal. It's a symbol of refreshment, a symbol that begins to create that kind of space in my life as it reminds me to pause and be restored.

As your spiritual practice for today, choose something that might serve as an everyday icon for you. It might be something that you already use that you can now repurpose—like one of the chairs in your living room, or a certain coffee mug, piece of pottery, or scarf. You could choose one corner of a room to set up a small table with a prayer cloth and a candle, or put together a basket with your Bible, a blank book to use as a journal, and a pen.

If you are drawn to the natural world, think of choosing a rock or a piece of driftwood, a potted plant, a vase for fresh flowers, or even the apple tree outside your kitchen window. Your everyday icon might be something that you leave in one place, like the coffee set that I leave on my desk; or you might choose something to carry with you throughout the day or even when traveling, like the cross-shaped bookmark given to me by a friend.

What might serve as a symbol of refreshment for you? What draws your heart and your mind to dwell on God? What gives

In the world of pro sports, an athlete can't expect to win a game just by getting dressed and getting out there. He has to practice, to work out and condition himself—more than once, more than twice—on a regular basis. She can't expect to win a game, or even lose with dignity, without practice. So too in our spiritual lives. If we want to be prepared for the inevitable challenges that will come our way, we will benefit from spiritual practice.

you a sense of space? A picture that's already hanging in your hallway, the swing in your backyard, a figurine on your mantel, an empty bowl just waiting to be filled. Anything might serve as an everyday icon as long as it's something you will see frequently throughout the day.

The creative and spiritual possibilities are as endless as your imagination, as uniquely personal as God's call in your life. Something may come to mind immediately, or feel free to think about it through the rest of the day. Take even more time if you wish by starting with something now and adding to it as the days go by. Look around you. Consider the possibilities. Make your choice, and then place your everyday icon where it can remind you to pause and be renewed. Allow God to create that space in you.

2

Slowing Down

Be still before the LORD, and wait patiently for him. . . .
Psalm 37:7

Our church camp is about an hour's drive from where we
live—past houses and storefronts to get to the highway,
past farmland and more city, through another small town and
past trees and more trees, until we finally make the last turn
onto the gravel road, past the houses for camp staff and up to
the main lodge.

There isn't a lot of traffic on that last stretch of highway
just before the camp, so we travel easily and at full speed, so
absorbed in our conversation that we almost miss the final turn.
But once the turn is made, we slow way down—in part because
of the gravel road, in part because of the sign that says SLOW,
and in part because slowing down is part of what it means to
go on retreat.

If we are to retreat in daily life, we also need to slow down.
When I'm working every day and out several evenings in a row;
when I do my errands on the fly, from home to the dry cleaners
to the hardware store to the credit union to the grocery store
and home again; when I drive an hour each way to see my
mother at least once or sometimes two or three times a week
when she's been ill—all these things that I love, need, and want
to do can make my life seem much too fast.

Parents with children at home have another whole constella-
tion of places to go and things to do. Students juggle school and

25

work, life at home or in the dorm, and connecting with their friends. Retired people tell me they are busy, too, some even busier than when they were employed full time. Even those who may feel as if they have too much time on their hands need to slow down—if not from too many activities, then from their own anxious thoughts and the many questions they face about their future. After all, slowing down on retreat is not only about slowing down in a physical way, but slowing down our restless spirits.[1]

The spiritual value of slowing down

One day a man named Jairus came to Jesus with a desperate plea for his daughter who was ill and near death. So Jesus went with him, surrounded by the disciples and by a large crowd, all pressing in on him and hurrying him along to heal Jairus's daughter.

While they were still on the way, Jesus suddenly turned to the crowd and asked, "Who touched my clothes?" At first the disciples were confused. Weren't they all in a hurry to reach the girl who was so dangerously ill? Couldn't Jesus see that the crowd was pressing in on him from all sides? Why then would he slow down to ask, "Who touched me?"

In their hurry, no one else had noticed that a woman in the crowd had touched Jesus' cloak and had been healed of her disease. But when Jesus felt the divine exercise of God's power, he slowed down to speak to her. Yes, Jairus's daughter was seriously ill. Yes, Jesus was urgently needed and in a hurry to go to her. But there was also time enough to slow down, time enough to call this woman out of the crowd, time enough to give her a word of healing and blessing. Only then was Jesus ready to continue on and restore Jairus's daughter as well.[2]

---

1. For more on "time-sickness," a term coined by American physician Larry Dossey, see Carl Honoré, *In Praise of Slow: How a Worldwide Movement Is Challenging the Cult of Speed* (Toronto: Random House of Canada, 2004), 3.
2. Mark 5:22-43.

Another time, Jesus received word from Mary and her sister, Martha, that their brother Lazarus had fallen ill. But instead of hurrying to help his good friend, Jesus stayed where he was for two extra days. By the time he arrived at their home, Lazarus had died and had already been in the tomb for four days; the house was full of mourners; and both sisters were convinced that Jesus had arrived too late. If only Jesus had been there, Lazarus would not have died! But what seemed too late to Mary and Martha and to all those who were with them proved to be just the right time for Jesus as he went to the tomb, had the stone rolled away, and called Lazarus back to life.[3]

In both stories, slowing down was not an unfortunate delay or some kind of distraction from Jesus' "real" mission. Instead, slowing down was a sign of Jesus' attention to the Spirit. Slowing down formed part of the rhythm of his life. It became a teachable moment for his disciples to rely on God's power instead of their own limited vision and abilities. It bore fruit in ministry to others as Jesus healed the woman in the crowd, as he went on to restore Jairus's daughter to full health, as he brought comfort to Mary and Martha, as he raised Lazarus from the dead. For Jesus, slowing down meant time enough for each one and time to give glory to God.

> In the Psalms, those who are anxious over personal attacks and injustice are admonished to slow down. Instead of giving way to worry or endlessly venting their anger or acting rashly, they are to "be still before the Lord, and wait patiently for him" (Psalm 37:7a). On a world scale, in the face of civil unrest and war, the nations are told, "Be still, and know that I am God! I am exalted among the nations, I am exalted in the earth" (Psalm 46:10).

Journaling as slowing down

For me, keeping a journal is one way of slowing down. While some may think of journaling as writing, I find that it is

---

3. John 11:1-45.

both more and less than that. In a published piece of writing like this book, it's important to pay attention to spelling, grammar, word choice, a consistent tone of voice, using a mix of shorter and longer sentences for interest, writing in paragraphs to help readers follow along. All of these elements—and many more—have a role in communicating effectively with readers in a public setting.

But in private writing, none of those things matter. No one else but me needs to understand my grocery list, so I can write *pb* for peanut butter and not worry if I misspell *asparagus*. No one else needs to understand my notes to myself. One time I made an outline for a short presentation—just a few notes scribbled out quickly on a half-sheet of paper—and someone looking over my shoulder asked in all seriousness, "Is that Chinese?" No, it was actually English, but so illegible it didn't make sense to anyone else! But that didn't matter, because my outline was meant as private writing just for me.

Journaling is a form of private writing—with more spiritual depth than a grocery list, but still private—not a public expression like writing a book, or a letter to the editor, or an essay for school, or a report for work. Journaling is between you and God, for your eyes only. Forget about trying to do it "right." Forget about spelling. Forget about complete sentences or getting the noun and verb to agree. Forget about nouns and verbs. In journaling, we can safely ignore the normal conventions of writing because it's private writing for personal reflection and not meant to be shared or understood by others.

So journaling is "less" than writing, and yet it is also much more. Journaling is thinking on paper, praying, drawing, doodling, making a list, writing a letter, jotting down notes, taking a photograph, pouring out your heart, crying, laughing, preserving memories, problem solving, asking questions.[4] It can be

---

4. Other forms of journaling include random note taking throughout the day; recording your dreams; dialogue journaling with yourself and with Scripture;

happy or sad or angry, just like your life. It can mean different colored pens for different moods. It can mean collecting sayings by other people or cutting out a cartoon from the newspaper or saving a card from a friend. It's possible to "journal" in a notebook, a file folder, a shoebox, on a scrap of paper, on a computer.

These days I most often journal by hand in a clothbound book that I keep on my bedside table. But I also journal on computer, and I keep a file folder for ticket stubs, cards, and other keepsakes. These are three different forms of private journal keeping.[5] My handwritten journal tends to be the most

---

Choosing a journal

There are many different kinds of journals: the standard blank book either lined (great for writing lists) or unlined (maybe better for drawing/diagramming); with a regular binding (that lies flat) or spiral bound (that allows the book to be folded over easily, although I sometimes find the spiral binding gets in my way); larger or smaller (easier to carry throughout the day); possibly dated (to encourage daily use, although you can freely ignore the dates if you don't journal every day); with or without Scripture verses, quotations, or other prompts.

If you prefer to journal on screen, you might try journaling software, such as LifeJournal, which comes in different versions for Christians, writers, and other special-interest groups, with helpful prompts, a personal timeline for major events, a daily pulse to track your mood or other life trends of your choosing (see www.lifejournal.com).

Taking the time to choose a journal that you like can make it easier for you to enjoy journaling, but don't confuse making a good choice with procrastination. If you find yourself unable to decide, or if you just never seem to get around to it, then simply start with any kind of notebook you might have at home, or even a single sheet of paper. Journaling is not so much about the kind of journal you choose, but how you use it.

---

keeping a diary; outlining discovery tasks to learn more about a particular subject. These are suggested by Ron Delbene with Herb Montgomery in *Alone with God: A Guide for a Personal Retreat* (Minneapolis, MN: Winston Press, 1984), 25–29.

5. Some might think of blogging and social networking as forms of journaling since they may appear to be quite personal and self-reflective, but these are also very public.

personal, my computer journal more about writing, my file folder more for things too big to paste into my handwritten journal. There's an overlap between them all too, with personal reflections turning up in my computer journal and writing appearing in my personal journal, and the same subject sometimes surfacing in all three.

In his book *Can You Drink the Cup?* Henri Nouwen writes, "Half of living is reflection on what is being lived."[6] I can't do that well at full speed. Instead, I physically and mentally slow down by sitting at my computer, or slow down even further to write with pen in hand. Thinking and praying on paper are ways of reflecting on my life. Diagramming my thoughts helps me flesh out my ideas and see new connections. A magazine from my local health food store says that "daily journaling is therapeutic."[7] An advertisement for a book on journaling says, "Learn to use journal writing to transform your life and live more authentically than ever before."[8] In addition to these many benefits, journaling also becomes spiritual practice as I bring my journaling before God and pause to listen for God's voice.

The writing of the prophet Jeremiah has been described as "journal-like"[9] as he makes his confession and complaints to God. Many of the Psalms also read like personal journal entries: "O Lord, in the morning you hear my voice; in the morning I plead my case to you, and watch,"[10] and "O God, you are my God, I seek you, my soul thirsts for you; my flesh faints for you, as in a dry and weary land where there is no water."[11] Following

6. Henri J. M. Nouwen, *Can You Drink the Cup?* (Notre Dame, IN: Ave Maria Press, 1996), 26.
7. Lily Dawn Robertson, "Listening for Quiet" in *Alive* (Richmond, BC: Alive Health Centre, February 2010), 124.
8. Quality Paperback Book Club ad for Stephanie Dowrick, *Creative Journal Writing* (Crows Nest, NSW, Australia: Allen & Unwin, 2007).
9. Jan Johnson, *Spiritual Disciplines Companion* (Downers Grove: InterVarsity Press, 2009), 213.
10. Psalm 5:3.
11. Psalm 63:1.

Been there, done that—
for those who "hate" journaling

Just as "one size fits all" doesn't really fit everyone, so also journaling may not be a good fit for everyone. Before you dismiss it too quickly though, ask yourself why you don't like journaling. Is it too much writing? (Try a picture journal instead, with your own sketches or photos or pictures cut from magazines.) Do you find it boring? (Try one of the variations below.) Do you have concerns about confidentiality? (Keep your journal in a safe place at home instead of carrying it around with you.) Is journaling just too slow? (Well, that's actually the point!)

If you're still not convinced, that's entirely okay. But why not give journaling another try anyway? You may not immediately love every spiritual practice, but if you allow yourself to experiment, if you allow yourself to be uncomfortable at times, you may find that what you don't like at first actually grows on you.

Some variations to try:

• Start with a to-do list since it's often easier to begin with something concrete; then move on to reflect on why these things are important to you.

• Instead of writing line after line, try a cluster diagram, with a main idea in the center of the page and related ideas branching out.

• Use prompts like your everyday icon or other object, a verse of Scripture, or simply review your day.

• If you are using this book in a group, try a group journal, where one person writes something and then passes it on. When it's your turn, you can read what others have written as a source of inspiration for your own journal entry. Agree to give each person a day or more when it's their turn, and keep all entries confidential.

• If you still don't like journaling, feel free to set it aside and try it again some other time.

the birth of Jesus, after hearing that angels had appeared to the shepherds, Mary, the mother of Jesus, "treasured all these words and pondered them in her heart."[12] She may not have written anything down—may not even have been able to read or write— but in journal-like fashion, Mary took time for personal reflection and wonder at God's work in her own life and in the world.

---

12. Luke 2:19.

Sacred pause: slow down and be uniquely you

As you deliberately slow down, close your eyes, and take two or three slow, deep breaths. When you feel centered, open your eyes, and take your journal if you have one, or some other piece of paper if you don't, and consider the everyday icon that you have chosen (see chapter 1). Why did you choose it? Where have you placed it? Has it served to remind you to take time for yourself and for God? Why or why not?

In a world of fast food and speed dating, I suppose it's possible to journal in a hurry too. But take your time with these questions. They're designed for reflection, not interrogation, and not meant to be rushed. The blank page is not a rebuke to get busy writing, but an invitation to linger over your thoughts. Jot down ideas as they come to you. If something unrelated comes to mind that you'd rather focus on, feel free to follow it instead. Doodle on your page. Sketch a picture. Make a list, or draw a diagram. Sometimes I just write down the date—"just checking in." If you find it difficult to sit still even for a few moments, set a timer if you must, or listen to some music during this time.

In a course I taught on journaling, the first practical exercise offered several different options: (1) Read Psalm 121, and reflect on what way(s) this psalm describes your own life. (2) Write a prayer about whatever is on your mind and heart today. (3) Or come up with your own idea. In the sharing time afterward, one member of the class who had never journaled before said that she didn't know what to do, so she tried to write out the psalm in the German that she had learned as a child. It wasn't at all something that I would have thought of, but it was something uniquely hers as she spent that time in contemplation and reflection before God.

That's part of the beauty of journaling—your journal will not be like anyone else's journal. And your own journaling practice may not be the same for you from day to day. Some days you may find yourself journaling spontaneously, so absorbed in what you are doing that you lose track of time. Other days you may need something to prompt you—a verse of Scripture, a quote from a book, or one of the journaling prompts included in this book. For journaling as slowing down, you don't need to write a lot, and you don't need to feel pressured to do it in a certain way. Just take a deep breath, and slow down.

3

Becoming Quiet

For God alone my soul waits in silence;
from him comes my salvation.
He alone is my rock and my salvation, my fortress;
I shall never be shaken.
Psalm 62:1-2

A friend of mine has furnished her living room with hospitality in mind. A comfortable sofa and chairs face one another across a low coffee table, everything arranged for sharing good coffee and good conversation. But every morning, she deliberately turns one of the chairs away from the others so it faces the window that looks out on her yard and toward the morning light. She says good-bye to her husband as he leaves for work, then makes a pot of her favorite Earl Grey tea, prepares a slice of toast, and settles down in her special chair. She savors the steaming fragrance of her tea, watches for sparrows and hummingbirds in her garden, enjoys her cat purring on her lap, reads, prays, or writes in her journal. "It's the whole experience that quiets my soul in the morning," she says. "It takes just a second, but that's my spiritual discipline—turning my chair to be available for God."

Listening into the silence

When Elijah was fleeing for his life from King Ahab and his wife, Jezebel, his soul was anything but quiet. He felt utterly alone in remaining faithful to God's covenant, and his distress was so great that he even asked God to take away his life rather than allow him to fall into the hands of the royal couple. But God answered his desperate prayer in another way; instead of taking his life, God gave him rest, provided food and water, and supplied him with enough strength to make it all the way to Mount Horeb, where Elijah found shelter in a cave. There God confronted him with a question: "What are you doing here, Elijah?" With all his fears for himself and for his people, Elijah struggled to answer. Then God said, "Go out and stand on the mountain before the LORD, for the LORD is about to pass by." Outside, there was a great wind storm, followed by an earthquake, followed by fire, but God was not in any of those. It was only afterward, in the sound of "sheer silence" that God spoke again, "What are you doing here, Elijah?"[1]

What is the sound of "sheer silence"? Can we hear silence? Is it the voice of God? Some English versions translate this as "a still small voice,"[2] or "a gentle whisper,"[3] or "a sound. Thin. Quiet."[4] These might seem to make more sense. After all, we can at least hear a small voice or a gentle whisper or a thin sound, and it's not clear what the sound of sheer silence might be. Yet, I prefer the more ambiguous expression for its poetry and for its sense of mystery; we don't really know what Elijah experienced alone on the mountain.

So what is silence? Some might say it's an absence of sound, an absence of communication. But I am intrigued by American composer and philosopher John Cage who says, "There is no such thing as silence."[5] Even in Harvard University's anechoic chamber—designed to absorb any sound from within, and soundproof from without—where the composer expected to

---

1. 1 Kings 19:1-18.
2. King James Version.
3. New International Version.
4. Common English Bible.
5. John Cage, *Silence: Lectures and Writings* (Middletown, CT: Wesleyan University Press, 1961), 191.

experience only silence, he found that he could still hear the sound of his own blood circulation and nervous system. As John Cage discovered, what we call silence is actually full of sound.

In his experimental approach to music, one of Cage's most well-known and most controversial pieces is *4'33"* a composition in three movements where not a single note is played. When performed by a full symphony, both conductor and all of the musicians remain apparently motionless. After the first movement, there is the usual page-turning, coughing, throat-clearing, and rustling from the audience, and when the conductor wipes his brow, everyone laughs. The tension continues to build as conductor and musicians remain apparently motionless again for the second movement, then the third, as each cough from the audience, each small sound in the concert hall seems magnified, and at the end of the piece there is an explosion of applause as the tension is at last released.

To some, *4'33"* may seem absurd. Why would anyone sit through a performance piece where nothing happens, where the instruments are silent and the musicians motionless? Is this some kind of farce, like the emperor who was convinced he was wearing the finest garments when in fact he had no clothes? To others, *4'33"* is a profound experience—at once uniquely personal as each person hears and experiences the piece in a different way each time as the sounds in their environment become the "music" they hear, and yet it is also a communal experience as everyone present is focused on listening into the silence.

I imagine that Elijah felt quite absurd standing on the mountain looking for God. What was he doing there? Was it some kind of cruel joke to be fleeing for his life only to find himself in the middle of a storm so violent that the rocks were shattering around him? And yet after the storm, after the earthquake, after the fire, Elijah had a profound experience of silence that allowed him to quiet his soul, to hear God, and to refocus.

Silence speaks volumes

In Scripture and in our own personal experience, we know that silence can actually communicate a lot. Sitting silently holding the hand of someone who is dying can communicate comfort. Standing in silence after a long hike up a mountain may say something about the breathtaking effort it took to get there as well as the breathtaking beauty of the 360-degree view. At times, silence may indicate agreement or resistance, confusion or anger, awkwardness or intimacy, admiration or dismay.

Journal Prompt:

Describe a time of comfortable silence. Describe a time of silence that was awkward. What made the difference for you?

When Jesus and his disciples arrive in Capernaum, Jesus asks them, "What were you arguing about on the way?" and the disciples are silent, perhaps embarrassed and feeling guilty, since they had been arguing about which of them was the greatest.[6] When religious leaders disapprove of Jesus healing on the Sabbath, Jesus confronts them with a question, "Is it lawful to do good or to do harm on the Sabbath, to save life or to kill?" Their refusal to answer is a hostile silence.[7] Before the high priest, Jesus' silence communicates his dignity and refusal to play into the hands of his accusers.[8]

When the psalmist is silent about his sin and refuses to confess it before God, he is tormented by his dishonesty with himself and with his Lord: "While I kept silence, my body wasted away through my groaning all day long. For day and night your hand was heavy upon me; my strength was dried up as by the heat of summer."[9] In this case and elsewhere, silence was a sign of distress.[10]

6. Mark 9:33-34.
7. Mark 3:1-6; cf. Luke 14:1-6.
8. Matthew 26:59-63a.
9. Psalm 32:3-4.
10. Psalm 39:1-3.

More positively, silence can also be a sign of reverence, as Moses and the priests direct the people, "Keep silence and hear, O Israel! This very day you have become the people of the LORD your God."[11] Later prophets also urge the people to be silent in reverence and awe before God: "Be silent, all people, before the LORD; for he has roused himself from his holy dwelling."[12] The prophet Habakkuk addresses this more broadly to the whole earth: "But the LORD is in his holy temple; let all the earth keep silence before him!"[13] In the book of Revelation, there is silence even in heaven as the Lamb opens the seventh seal.[14]

One day while Jesus was praying with Peter, John, and James, Jesus' appearance was suddenly changed. His face shone with a new light and his clothes became so bright that it hurt to look at him. Then Moses and Elijah also appeared and spoke with Jesus about his coming death. The three disciples were so overcome that Peter blurted out, "Master, it is good for us to be here; let us make three dwellings, one for you, one for Moses, and one for Elijah." But as he was still speaking, a cloud descended on them, and the voice of God said, "This is my Son, my Chosen; listen to him!"

When the voice had spoken and the cloud lifted, Moses and Elijah had disappeared. Afterward, the disciples kept silent about what had happened—perhaps with mixed feelings of amazement, uncertainty, fear, and awe, not knowing how to think about the whole experience or how to put it adequately into words. After Jesus' death and resurrection, they would be better able to speak of what they had seen and heard, but for now silence gave them time to reflect on their experience and what it might mean, to wrestle with their own thoughts and questions.[15]

---

11. Deuteronomy 27:9.
12. Zechariah 2:13; cf. Zephaniah 1:7.
13. Habakkuk 2:20.
14. Revelation 8:1.
15. Luke 9:28-36; cf. Matthew 17:1-9 where Jesus tells the disciples not to tell anyone about their vision.

When God is silent

In Scripture, God's silence appears most often as a sign of distance or anger. So the psalmist prays in his distress, "You have seen, O LORD; do not be silent! O Lord, do not be far from me!" (Psalm 35:22). The prophet Isaiah pleads on behalf of his people, "After all this, will you restrain yourself, O LORD? Will you keep silent, and punish us so severely?" (Isaiah 64:12). As Jesus himself prayed on the cross, "My God, my God, why have you forsaken me?" (Mark 15:34).

Such anguish over God's apparent silence and abandonment is part of what St. John of the Cross meant by the "dark night of the soul." In the midst of spiritual discouragement and crisis, when it seems as if God is silent and far away, we may feel as if all is lost. But what may seem futile is really part of the journey, as God continues to work in our lives even if perhaps in unseen ways. God says, "'I will never leave you or forsake you.' So we can say with confidence, 'The Lord is my helper; I will not be afraid. What can anyone do to me?'" (Hebrews 13:5-6). Jesus himself says, "I am with you always, to the end of the age" (Matthew 28:20).

As the disciples were discovering, a lot can happen even in silence. When we pray and can't seem to get an answer, when we try to work for change but things seem to remain the same, when we try to teach our kids to make good choices but they don't seem to be listening, we may think that nothing is happening, that God is silent. But just as John Cage's *4'33"* demonstrates that silence is actually full of sound, so God continues to speak to us and to work in our lives through Scripture, prayer, and in our own hearts, even in the silences we may experience today.

Practicing silence

Quaker minister and retreat leader J. Brent Bill describes the Quaker practice of holding silence this way: "Silence is something we do, not something done to us. It is a participatory act. It engages our heart, mind, soul, and body in listening for the voice of the Beloved."[16] What's more:

16. J. Brent Bill, *Holy Silence: The Gift of Quaker Spirituality* (Brewster, MA: Paraclete Press, 2005), 9.

> Silence begins with expectation—the expectation of
> encountering God. Holy Silence is just not an exercise in
> clearing your thoughts or finding a little peace and quiet.
> Peace and quiet may come, but they will come as a result of
> having been in the presence of the ever-living ever-loving
> Christ. One incentive for getting away from earthly noise
> and human voices is to hear the Voice from Heaven.[17]

Holding silence together is part of Quaker worship—a time to wait in expectation, a time to be drawn closer to God and to others, a time to be fully aware and to focus attention on God. Such times of corporate silence can also be powerful in a retreat setting, where participants might spend a day or several days in silence even during their common meals. One friend makes an eight-day silent retreat every year as part of her spiritual practice.

But practicing silence is not only for Quaker meetings, retreat houses, or other group settings. When I'm home alone, I can resist the temptation to turn on the television or listen to the radio. I can leave my earbuds at home when I go for a walk, enjoying the sounds of children playing, a dog barking, the wind in the trees, even the traffic, while I silently give thanks for the day and listen beyond those everyday sounds for God.

As J. Brent Bill points out, observing silence is not only about finding peace and quiet in a noisy world. That's part of it—but even more, it's discovering that God speaks in the silence, that silence releases me to be myself before God and to pour out my heart in confession, worry, joy, shame, frustration, or whatever else I may be carrying. Silence allows me to appreciate God in a new way, and allows for a depth of intimacy that may even make me uncomfortable at times.

In the fourteenth century, Christian mystic and theologian Meister Eckhart wrote, "Nothing in all creation is so like God as silence."[18] I don't fully understand what he means by that, but

---

17. Ibid., 70.
18. Ibid., 16.

as I get used to silence, I find that I also deepen my relationship with God.

The wisdom literature of the Bible encourages me: there is "a time to keep silence, and a time to speak."[19] The prophet Isaiah, for all his many words, also writes, "For thus said the LORD GOD, the Holy One of Israel: In returning and rest you shall be saved; in quietness and in trust shall be your strength."[20] In times of personal distress, the psalmist takes refuge in silence: "When you are disturbed, do not sin; ponder it on your beds, and be silent."[21] In quiet contemplation of the night sky, the psalmist asks, "When I look at your heavens, the work of your fingers, the moon and the stars that you have established; what are human beings that you are mindful of them, mortals that you care for them?"[22]

When I sit quietly with my journal, like the psalmist I also sit with my questions. Who am I, that God cares for me? Who am I as a child of God? As I think about my day, I might consider, What do I need to say yes to? Where do I need to say no? Where do I need further discernment?

As God asked Elijah, "What are you doing here?" I also find myself asking, What am I doing here? It's a big-picture, existential, what-is-the-meaning-of-life kind of question that can also be personal, as in What am I doing in this job? What am I doing living in this neighborhood? What am I doing in my family life? What am I doing in my church? And like Elijah, as I face my questions and listen into the silence, I wait for God.

Sacred pause: experiment with silence

As a silent spiritual practice, try one or more of the following:

(1) Put down this book, and spend some time in silence outdoors. Stand still and close your eyes. What do you feel? Is

---

19. Ecclesiastes 3:7.
20. Isaiah 30:15.
21. Psalm 4:4.
22. Psalm 8:3-4.

there a cooling breeze, a light rain, sun, or snowflakes? What do you smell? Is it the soft scent of lilacs, the fumes of car exhaust, the neighbors' barbecue, or something else? What do you hear? A mower in the distance, a bird song, a passing car, someone laughing, your own heartbeat? Listen for the silence between the sounds. Listen for God.

(2) Spend time in silence with your journal. Consider the question that God asked Elijah, "What are you doing here?" What do you need to leave behind to enter into silence? What do you expect to receive during a time of silence? What will you want to come back to? Write or draw if you wish, or simply sit with your questions.

(3) Read Psalm 62:5-8. What thoughts or situations might distract you from silence with God? How do you call yourself back to silence? What is on your heart at this moment? Pour it out before God, who is your rock and refuge.

A silent exercise: Psalm 62

Psalm 62 begins with the psalmist waiting for God: "For God alone my soul waits in silence." Then after this heartfelt expression of confidence in God, the psalmist turns his attention to his opponents: "How long will you assail a person, will you batter your victim, all of you?" Fortunately his digression doesn't last long, as he brings his distress to God and recalls himself again to silence:

**For God alone my soul waits in silence,
for my hope is from him.
He alone is my rock and my salvation,
my fortress; I shall not be shaken.
On God rests my deliverance and my honor;
my mighty rock, my refuge is in God.
Trust in him at all times, O people;
pour out your heart before him;
God is a refuge for us
(Psalm 62:5-8).**

4

Engaging Scripture

Your word is a lamp to my feet
and a light to my path.
Psalm 119:105

Most often, I think of spiritual practice as its own rationale. Creating space, slowing down, and becoming quiet all have their own intrinsic value in a world that seems crowded with competing and ever-increasing demands pushing and pulling me in different directions. I value the space simply to be myself before God; in the fast pace of everyday living, I need to slow down for its own sake and to catch my breath; with all the noise from within and without, I long for the peace and clarity of becoming quiet. These things are valuable in and of themselves. Why create space? Simply to have some space. Why slow down? Simply to slow down. Why become quiet? To become quiet. These qualities need no other justification.

And yet, if I banish the spirit of busyness, what will take its place? Jesus tells the story of an "unclean spirit" that had gone out of a person but couldn't find another resting place. So the spirit decided to go back to its previous home, and found it "swept and put in order," ready for the unclean spirit's return along with seven other unclean spirit friends. As a result, the story concludes, "the last state of that person is worse than the first."[1]

Without getting caught up in a debate over the existence or identity of "unclean spirits," I understand that Jesus is speaking

---

1. Luke 11:24-26.

about the nature of our inner life. To that end, if all I do is sweep my life clean, is it possible that I might end up worse than at first? For all the intrinsic value of creating space and slowing down and becoming quiet, what then will fill the resulting vacancies? If John Cage is right that there is no such thing as silence, what then will fill the silence when I become quiet? What new temptations, fears, doubts, worries, loneliness, distractions, restlessness, or other "spirits" might come to take up residence, and how will I face these?

In light of these questions, I understand that creating space, slowing down, and becoming quiet are more than simply ends in themselves. Yes, they have their own rationale and their own intrinsic value, but like the first three movements of many a symphony, they also prepare the way for a fourth movement. That's why this book is more than just the first three chapters; they open up to further spiritual practice like reading Scripture or praying, fasting or having fun, valuing relationships, giving, confessing, living more simply. Practicing these and other spiritual disciplines means that my life is not simply swept clean and standing empty, but filled in positive and life-giving ways by a fourth, fifth, sixth, and further movement of God's Spirit.

Grounded in Scripture

The first three movements of creating space, slowing down, and becoming quiet have already been grounded in Scripture as the foundational text for Christian spiritual practice. Each chapter begins with a quotation from the book of Psalms, which Martin Luther called "a little Bible"[2] because it so beautifully and briefly contains everything found elsewhere in the Bible. What's more, Scripture is woven into each chapter of this book, with the experience of the psalmists, the life of Jesus, his

---

2. Martin Luther, "Preface to Psalms," in *The Prefaces to the Early Editions of Martin Luther's Bible*, T.A. Readwin, ed. (London: Hatchard & Co., 1863), 44.

teaching and stories, the examples of the prophet Elijah, the apostle Paul, and other biblical figures. Scripture gives shape to spiritual practice, providing the narrative and theological ground to inform, guide, nourish, enrich, and strengthen us.

> **One does not live by bread alone, But by every word that comes from the mouth of God (Matthew 4:4).**

This central role of Scripture is demonstrated in Jesus' own life and experience. As he inaugurates his public ministry, he reads the scroll of Isaiah, applying the words of the prophet to himself:

> The Spirit of the Lord is upon me, because he has anointed me to bring good news to the poor.
> He has sent me to proclaim release to the captives and recovery of sight to the blind,
> to let the oppressed go free, to proclaim the year of the Lord's favor.[3]

When he faces temptation three times in the wilderness, Jesus responds three times with words of Scripture. "One does not live by bread alone, but by every word that comes from the mouth of God."[4] "Do not put the Lord your God to the test."[5] "Worship the Lord your God, and serve only him."[6]

Jesus' teaching is filled with references to Scripture, especially in his Sermon on the Mount, where he addresses anger, lust, lying, revenge, love of neighbor and enemy, giving, prayer, fasting, and other subjects all in the context of Old Testament teaching. "Do not think that I have come to abolish the law or the prophets," he says, "I have come not to abolish but to fulfill. For truly I tell you, until heaven and earth pass away, not one

---

3. Luke 4:18-19; cf. Isaiah 61:1-2.
4. Matthew 4:4; cf. Deuteronomy 8:3.
5. Matthew 4:7; cf. Deuteronomy 6:16.
6. Matthew 4:10; cf. Deuteronomy 6:13.

letter, not one stroke of a letter, will pass from the law until all is accomplished."[7]

Even his terrible suffering and death on the cross are grounded in Scripture,[8] and after his resurrection he would explain to his disciples "the things about himself in all the scriptures."[9] Clearly, Jesus knew the Scriptures—not in any casual or superficial way, but so thoroughly and deeply that Scripture shaped his teaching, his identity, mission, and ministry, his life, death, and resurrection.

For Jesus, Scripture was the Law, the Prophets, and the Writings of the Hebrew Scriptures—what Christians today call the Old Testament. As Jesus' followers then wrote about his life and ministry, as they wrote letters of encouragement and instruction to the Christian communities that were being formed, their writings also became recognized as Scripture and arranged in what we now know as the New Testament.

> Let the word of Christ dwell in you richly;
> teach and admonish one another in all wisdom;
> and with gratitude in your hearts sing psalms, hymns, and spiritual songs to God
>
> (Colossians 3:16).

Over the years, both Old and New Testaments have been sources of inspiration, spiritual guidance, comfort, and practical wisdom for many people around the world. At the same time, they have also been misquoted and misused in many ways to justify war and oppression, to destroy cultures, to promote racism and hatred of all kinds. The history of the Bible has been tarnished again and again by those who have misused and abused it for their own ends.

And yet Scripture has endured through it all and still declares, "All scripture is inspired by God and is useful for teaching, for reproof, for correction, and for training in righteousness, so

---

7. Matthew 5:17-18.
8. Isaiah 53; Psalm 22.
9. Luke 24:27.

that everyone who belongs to God may be proficient, equipped for every good work."[10] Rather than abandoning Scripture to those who misuse it or getting tied up in knots over various interpretations and misinterpretations, there's all the more reason to read Scripture carefully, to study and immerse ourselves in it as Jesus did, to be engaged by Scripture and know it deeply.

Shaped by Scripture

When the people of Israel returned to Jerusalem and Judah after their years of exile in Babylon, they held a day of celebration that began with reading Scripture together and ended with a great feast that was shared by all the people. Men, women, youth, and children all gathered together while Ezra the priest read from the law "from early morning until midday." As Ezra read, the people listened attentively; they stood as a sign of respect for God's Word; they responded by lifting their hands in praise to God, saying Amen, and bowing with their faces to the ground; they wept with emotion.

Ezra and his assistants helped them to understand the Scripture, encouraging them to celebrate and to move forward with rejoicing, obedience, and sharing with others. For the next day and for days afterward, the people continued to hear the reading of Scripture, to put it into practice, and to celebrate. It was an amazing time of being engaged and energized by the Word of God.[11]

I am especially struck by the reading of Scripture that went on for hours and lasted all morning long! How was it that the people seemed to remain fully engaged and not at all bored as I might imagine people responding today?

What a contrast to our own restlessness after listening to Scripture for just a few moments, as we stumble over unfamiliar

---

10. 2 Timothy 3:16-17.
11. Nehemiah 8:1-18.

names and unfamiliar places, or find our attention wandering when it seems a passage has become all too familiar. As a writer and preacher, I know how important it is to start with an interesting hook and connect it to Scripture. That advice appears in many writers' guidelines and is regularly taught in classes on preaching. Yet even though I often write or speak that way, something in me rebels, for it seems to assume that Scripture itself is not enough to grab and hold our attention.

Journal Prompt

What has been your experience with Scripture? Do you already have an established practice of reading the Bible? Why or why not?

For all that, I am convinced that Scripture *is* inherently interesting, that it has the power to engage and energize us today just as it did the people of Israel long ago. If we are bored or find our minds wandering, perhaps that has less to do with Scripture and more to do with the entertainment-seeking and over-stimulated age in which we live. As philosophy professor Mark Kingwell writes, "The bored are rather like the teenager who, standing before a well-stocked fridge, complains that there is never anything to eat."[12] When it comes to Scripture, the fridge is well stocked, and we can partake in any number of ways.

Perhaps one of the most common ways for us to engage Scripture is to read it in short sections. In my church, the sermon is often based on a passage of Scripture that is read during our time of worship—perhaps just a few verses, half a chapter, or more rarely a whole chapter of the Bible. For personal reading, many daily devotional books feature a short passage of Scripture for each day along with a few paragraphs of explanation. The story of Ezra and his assistants reading Scripture to the people is found in just such a short section in Nehemiah 8:1-18.

---

12. Mark Kingwell, "Warning: The Topic Today Is Boredom," in *Marginalia: A Cultural Reader* (Toronto: Penguin Books, 1999), 191.

But reading in short sections is just one way of reading Scripture. Another way is to recognize that the Bible is actually a collection of 66 different books—some are narratives that cover one or more generations of people, some are poetry, some are gospels on the life of Jesus, some are letters. Instead of plucking just eighteen verses from the middle of the book of Nehemiah to read about Ezra and the people of Israel, another option would be to begin with chapter one and read all thirteen chapters in order. With that context, Ezra's reading of the law can be seen as part of the much larger story of how the exiled people returned to Jerusalem and rebuilt the city and its walls. Instead of an isolated day of celebration, their holy day can be understood as a culmination of a whole series of events in the life of the people.

Still another way to read Scripture is to focus on a particular subject, by using a topical Bible that organizes Scripture under various headings such as peace, faith, heart, music, thanksgiving, or other topics of interest.[13] Or choose topics of your own, and look for key words in a Bible concordance, or simply keep your own list as you read, to get a sense of the breadth of Scriptural teaching on the topic of your choice.

These are just three ways of reading Scripture,[14] each one highlighting a different aspect of the text. Sometimes I concentrate on just one short section, which allows for a close reading, focusing on a particular situation or character. At other times, I choose to read through an entire book at once to get the big picture, deepening my understanding of Scripture in its context and guarding against a too narrow understanding. The richness and complexity of Scripture become even more evident when I read according to topic and gain a sense of the breadth of Scriptural teaching.

---

13. For example, John R. Kohlenberger III, gen. ed., *Zondervan NIV Nave's Topical Bible* (Grand Rapids: Zondervan, 1994), or other online versions.
14. *Lectio Divina*, literally "sacred reading," is another way of reading the Bible. See chapter 16, Praying Scripture.

It's also possible to combine all three ways of reading, like the time I read through the book of Psalms looking for all the names of God. I read the Psalms in short sections (spreading the longest Psalm 119 over two weeks), but I eventually read through the whole book, and when I was done I had my own topical list of names for God—Almighty, King, Most High, and other recurring titles that I could have looked up in a concordance; but I also discovered other less common names like "Stronghold,"[15] "God of my praise,"[16] and even "a God who has indignation every day"[17] that wouldn't have occurred to me. My reading was a rich experience that both deepened my love for the Psalms and led me to discover God in a new way.

So feel free to experiment: read a short section of Scripture, read an entire book, read according to topic, or do all three. Immersing ourselves in Scripture even for a few moments is a natural way of taking a break from our daily lives, for its narrative takes us into a world that's different from our own; its poetry gives voice to the cry of the human heart and lifts us beyond the routine of daily living.

Long ago, the writer to the Hebrews declared that "the word of God is living and active, sharper than any two-edged sword, piercing until it divides soul from spirit, joints from marrow; it is able to judge the thoughts and intentions of the heart."[18] In other words, it is not only that we read Scripture, but that Scripture itself has a way of reading us. That's the movement of God's Spirit, to engage and enliven us, to deepen, change, and shape us.

Sacred pause: (re)discover Scripture

If your reading of Scripture is already well established, you may prefer to carry on with your regular reading. But if you would

---

15. Psalm 94:22.
16. Psalm 109:1.
17. Psalm 7:11.
18. Hebrews 4:12.

like a change of pace, or if you are new to Bible reading, here
are several options for (re)discovering Scripture:

(1) For a topical approach, go back and reread the verses
from the Psalms that introduce each chapter of this book. How
is God revealed to you in these verses? What do they say to you
about rest and renewal? Is there a word or a phrase that you
might carry with you through the rest of your day? Another
option for a topical approach is to look up the Scripture references in the notes for this chapter and discover more about
what Scripture says about itself.

(2) To read a short section of
Scripture, begin with one of the
texts listed in the sidebar.

What is the main point of these
verses? Try to sum it up in your
own words in just one sentence.
How might you celebrate this or
put it into practice?

(3) To read an entire book, consider beginning with the gospel of
Mark since it focuses on the life
of Jesus, written with a minimum
of description and a maximum of
action. Notice the different charac-
ters: followers of Jesus, his family,
a woman healed of disease, a man

Suggested Scripture readings:

- **If you love poetry: Psalm 23**
- **If you love a good story: Acts 16:16-40**
- **If you're looking for encouragement: Isaiah 40:28-31**
- **If you're looking for practical advice: James 1:22-27**
- **On creation: Genesis 1:1-31**
- **On love: 1 Corinthians 13:1-13**
- **On reassurance: Psalm 139**
- **Jesus' Sermon on the Mount: Matthew 5:1–7:29**
- **God's presence always: Romans 8:31-39**
- **Praise: Psalm 103**
- **Prayer for help: Psalm 121**

who receives his sight, a crowd of hungry people. With whom do
you identify, and why? Imagine yourself in the story. Or consider
reading the book of James in one sitting, a practical book of just
five short chapters.

5

Praying It Like It Is

Give ear to my words, O LORD; give heed to my sighing.
Listen to the sound of my cry, my King and my God,
for to you I pray.
Psalm 5:1-2

As I entered the main lodge of our church camp, I immediately noticed the new banner hanging over our registration table as a sign of welcome: "COME AS YOU ARE"—large, dark letters on a wash of color, pine trees painted on one end, standing almost like exclamation marks. The banner reflected the informal nature of the camp and was meant to be an invitation, to give us freedom to be ourselves, to be authentic, to be real. And yet it made me wonder, Is it ever really possible to "come as you are" even in a camp setting?

All around me I saw people dressed pretty much alike—blue jeans, hoodies, sneakers. If camp was really "come as you are," how had everyone somehow managed to choose the same uniform? I too had deliberately chosen to wear casual clothes in keeping with the informal setting and the cool weather—my favorite black jeans, a T-shirt, a sweater, sneakers—not the dress-up clothes that I was planning to wear to a thirty-fifth wedding anniversary celebration later that afternoon. Those I had carefully stowed in the trunk of our car so I could change into them later. Even if I had felt like dressing up that morning, I wouldn't have worn my dressier skirt and jacket to the church retreat, and even if I felt more laid back in the afternoon, I wouldn't have worn my jeans to celebrate my friends' renewal of their wedding vows. I'm the same person in both situations, but what I choose to wear depends on the occasion. It's never exactly "come as you are."

> Do not worry about anything, but in everything by prayer and supplication with thanksgiving let your requests be made known to God. And the peace of God, which surpasses all understanding, will guard your hearts and your minds in Christ Jesus (Philippians 4:6-7).

But prayer is different. It's the one place that I can actually come as I am—whatever I am wearing, however I am feeling. I don't need to dress up or dress down, literally or figuratively. Prayer releases me from having to think about any of that. That's why prayer is one of my favorite sacred pauses. As Jesus says, "Come to me, all you that are weary and are carrying heavy burdens, and I will give you rest. Take my yoke upon you, and learn from me; for I am gentle and humble in heart, and you will find rest for your souls. For my yoke is easy, and my burden is light."[1] I can come to Jesus just as I am.

Our whole selves

I am encouraged by the example of the psalmists who came before God just as they were. They prayed when they were happy: "Bless the LORD, O my soul, and all that is within me, bless his holy name."[2] They prayed when they felt helpless and afraid: "Hear, O LORD, and be gracious to me! O LORD, be my helper!"[3] They prayed out their suffering: "My God, my God, why have you forsaken me? Why are you so far from helping me, from the words of my groaning?"[4] They prayed out their complaints and loneliness: "Turn to me and be gracious to

1. Matthew 11:28-30.
2. Psalm 103:1.
3. Psalm 30:10.
4. Psalm 22:1.

me, for I am lonely and afflicted. Relieve the troubles of my heart, and bring me out of my distress."[5] They even gave vent to their anger and desire for revenge: "O daughter Babylon, you devastator! Happy shall they be who pay you back what you have done to us! Happy shall they be who take your little ones and dash them against the rock!"[6] Theirs were not always nice prayers, not always "proper" prayers, not always prayers that I would feel comfortable praying, but they were honest prayers that revealed the depth of their relationship with God.

Journal Prompt

Write, draw, or diagram a "come as you are" prayer, telling God of your joy, frustration, or other experience.

In the early church, James writes to his brothers and sisters to encourage their honest prayers. "Are any among you suffering?" he asks. "They should pray." If anyone is cheerful, if anyone is sick, his encouragement is still the same—come as you are to God in prayer. We don't need to pretend that our lives are perfect, we don't need to hide our sickness or suffering; we can bring our disappointments, our sadness, our anger, our outrage to God. In the same breath, James reminds us that we can also turn to God with our good feelings, triumphs, and joys. When things are going well, when we feel strong and optimistic about life, God welcomes us in prayer then too. We can come to God at any time and in any way with our whole selves.[7]

As an example of prayer, James points to Elijah as "a human being like us." He says nothing about Elijah as a great prophet and leader, but as I read Elijah's story in the rest of the Bible, his prayer life seems superhuman. Elijah prayed for a boy who had fallen ill and had stopped breathing, and the boy revived. In a showdown with false prophets, Elijah prayed for God to answer,

---

5. Psalm 25:16-17.
6. Psalm 137:8-9.
7. James 5:13-14.

and God sent down fire that consumed the sacrifice that Elijah had prepared along with the stones of the altar and the water that had been poured around it. God sent fire, and there was soon nothing left of the sacrifice, stones, or water! Elijah prayed, and the boy who was dying or already dead, came back to life! As James also points out, Elijah prayed for no rain, and it didn't rain for three years and six months! Then Elijah prayed again, and the rains returned.[8]

My own prayer life is just not that spectacular. At other times, neither was Elijah's. Not long after these spectacular answers to prayer, Elijah was overwhelmed with loneliness and fear, and his prayers became mainly complaints to God. He was so afraid and depressed that he even prayed for God to take his life.[9] Perhaps that's part of what James means by Elijah being "a human being like us"; he experienced both highs and lows in his personal and spiritual life. He struggled with the same fears and doubts and dryness in prayer that we may sometimes experience. Yet Elijah kept praying. And so can we.

In *Memories of God*, Roberta Bondi tells her story of growing up and becoming a writer and professor of church history at Emory University in Atlanta, Georgia. The book is part memoir of her personal life and her academic interest in the early Christian church, but it's also part theological reflection as she describes how the earliest writers of the Christian church shaped her own prayer life. As a result, she says, "I was able to lay aside my modern assumptions about prayer. . . . I abandoned the notion that prayer is basically verbal petition and praise, and came to see that prayer is a sharing of the whole self and an entire life with God."[10]

There's nothing wrong with "petition and praise." Jesus himself taught his disciples to ask, seek, knock, as part of their

---

8. James 5:17-18; cf. 1 Kings 17, 18.
9. 1 Kings 19:4.
10. Roberta Bondi, *Memories of God: Theological Reflections on a Life* (Nashville: Abingdon Press, 1995), 33f.

relationship with God,[11] and he himself prayed with thanks-giving.[12] But imagine what it would be like if the only time anyone ever talked to you is when they wanted something: your kids only when they wanted a new toy; your brother-in-law only when he wanted to use your truck; your friends only when they wanted to borrow money. Even if they would always say thank you, would that be enough? So too, prayer goes deeper to "sharing of the whole self." That's how the psalmists prayed, and that's how James and Elijah prayed as well. They shared their whole selves with God—with words, yes, with petition and praise, but even more deeply with their hearts.

You don't always get what you want (you get something better)

If prayer means coming as we are and sharing our lives with God, then there is really no such thing as "unanswered" prayer. The apostle Paul writes of his own prayer life, how he asked God to remove a "thorn" from his life. He never reveals what it was—perhaps some physical ailment or a spiritual struggle. Whatever the identity of his particular thorn, he prayed fervently for release, yet still his thorn persisted.

On one level, you might say that Paul's prayer remained unanswered because he didn't get what he wanted. But clearly Paul understood God's answer: "My grace is sufficient for you, for power is made perfect in weakness."[13] Paul had his answer in God's presence, grace, and power in his life in spite of the thorn that continued to plague him.

Even while James insists on the importance and power of prayer, he also admits that we don't always get what we pray for. He says that sometimes we ask wrongly for things for our own

---

11. Matthew 7:7-11.
12. Mark 8:6; 14:22-25.
13. 2 Corinthians 12:7-9.

pleasure,[14] sometimes we need to exercise patience while we wait for our answer,[15] and sometimes we ask and don't receive because we simply don't recognize the answer when it comes.[16]

I've experienced each of these in my own prayer life. Like the time I prayed for resolution to a problem, but as it persisted, I gradually came to realize that I was praying mainly so that I would no longer be bothered by it—for my own pleasure, as James might say—and not out of genuine concern for all of the parties involved. I've prayed for peace—we've prayed for peace as a church many times and on behalf of many different parts of the world—and yet there is still great turmoil and suffering. Under such circumstances, patience is difficult, but I wonder, is it only we who are waiting, or is God also waiting, waiting for us to recognize our own complicity and to be convicted of our own responsibility to live in ways that make for peace? According to James, we need to be patient "until the coming of the Lord."[17]

Many times I've prayed for healing for others—and unlike Elijah who prayed and saved a young boy from death—my friends instead grew worse and, humanly speaking, passed on all too soon. Clearly they were not healed of their disease, but just as clearly I could see that they experienced great healing in their relationships with other people, they received forgiveness from any sins they may have committed, and they were able to pass on in peace. They were "saved" not in the narrow sense of physical healing, but in a much more profound way as their prayers and mine were answered in God's own way.

Even Jesus did not get all of his prayers answered in the way that we might expect. Not long before his arrest, Jesus prayed for the unity of his disciples, and for the future unity of the

---

14. James 4:1-3.

15. James 5:8-11.

16. James 5:15-16 says nothing of physical healing, but prayers for the sick are answered with forgiveness of sin and the prayer support of the Christian community.

17. James 5:7.

In 1529, Anna of Freiburg, Germany, was arrested, tortured, and sentenced to death for her radical Christian faith. She died by drowning and then her body was burned. One of her prayers survives from that time:

> Dear eternal, heavenly Father, I call upon Thee, from the depths of my heart; do not let me turn from Thee, but keep me in Thy truth unto my end. O God, keep my heart and mouth; guard me, that I may never separate from Thee, on account of impending sorrow and anguish, or any manner of distress; keep me cheerful and glad in my sufferings. . . . I commend myself to God and His church; may He be my Protector today, for His holy name's sake. O my Father, let it be done through Jesus Christ, Amen.
> —Thieleman J. van Braght, *Martyrs Mirror*, Joseph F. Sohm, tr. (Scottdale: Herald Press, 1950), 434–435.

In this prayer, Anna calls on God to be her Protector, and yet she was martyred for her faith. Note carefully what she prays for. In what way(s) did God answer her prayer?

church.[18] But instead of the unity he envisioned, one of his followers would betray him. Another would deny him. All would end up deserting him. Today, the church is fragmented into different denominations, and even individual local churches have trouble maintaining unity. Jesus' prayer then and now has not yet been fully answered. But there is still time "until the coming of the Lord," time for us to consider how we contribute to the unity of the church or detract from it, time to see the ways that Jesus' prayer is already being answered, time to be patient.

When the psalmists' prayers were not answered in the way or in the time that they expected, they freely voiced their impatience, frustration, and disappointment: "How long, O LORD? Will you hide yourself forever?"[19]—sometimes over and over again: "How long, O LORD? Will you forget me forever? How long will you hide your face from me? How long must I bear pain in my soul, and have sorrow in my heart all day long? How long shall my

18. John 17:20-21.
19. Psalm 89:46.

enemy be exalted over me?"[20] This too is part of prayer, part of what it means to come as we are before God, without pretense or any kind of self-censorship. God is strong enough, patient enough, faithful enough to take even our frustration and anger and transform them. In time, we may receive the answer that we seek. In time, we may realize as Jean Ingelow puts it: "I have lived to thank God that all my prayers have not been answered."[21] In the meantime, as we continue to wait and pray, pray and wait, we can continue to come to God with our whole selves.

Sacred pause: pray with body, mind, soul, and spirit

As human beings, we are body, mind, soul, and spirit, so to pray with our whole selves, we might also consider our posture when we pray. As a child, I learned to pray by folding my hands, bowing my head, and closing my eyes. Now as an adult, I most often pray with the palms of my hands facing up, ready to receive God's blessing. I often pray when I'm walking, or sometimes lying down, imagining myself resting in the palm of God's hand. The early church father Origen recommended standing with hands extended and eyes raised, since he believed the position of the body reflected the position of the soul.[22] Scripture describes many different physical postures for prayer: standing,[23] kneeling,[24] lying down,[25] head bowed,[26] eyes lowered,[27] eyes raised to heaven.[28]

---

20. Psalm 13:1-2.
21. Cited in Timothy Jones, *The Art of Prayer* (New York: Ballantine Books, 1997), 146.
22. Origen, *Origen On Prayer*, William A. Curtis, tr., Chapter XX, date unknown, Christian Classics Ethereal Library, http://www.ccel.org/ccel/origen/prayer.pdf.
23. Luke 18:13.
24. Luke 22:41; Acts 9:40; 20:36; 21:5.
25. Deuteronomy 9:18.
26. Genesis 24:26; Exodus 34:8; Psalm 35:13.
27. Luke 18:13.
28. Psalm 121:1; Mark 6:41; John 11:41; 17:1.

Take a moment to consider your own prayer posture both physically and spiritually. If prayer has already been part of your spiritual practice, what physical postures have you used most frequently? Do these mirror your spiritual attitude as the early church fathers maintained? If personal prayer is new to you, what might it mean for you to "come as you are" in prayer?

For your spiritual practice, think about sharing your whole self with God, and choose a physical stance that mirrors your attitude. Then spend a moment in God's presence—with words or without; in silence or speaking out loud; asking, seeking, knocking, or simply listening. God welcomes you to come as you are.

6

Getting Outside

For your steadfast love is before my eyes,
and I walk in faithfulness to you.
Psalm 26:3

In 1577, St. Teresa of Avila wrote *The Interior Castle*, which imagines the soul as a magnificent castle made of the clearest crystal and containing many mansions of prayer. She envisions prayer as union with God and describes both the sweetness of prayer as well as its struggle: the obstacles, distractions, and difficulties encountered by the soul that seeks God. While her focus is on this interior journey, she also recognizes that it is not entirely separate from our exterior circumstances and experiences. On difficulties in prayer, she speaks of "troubles both interior and exterior."[1] As a way of coping with inner anguish, she recommends performing "external works of charity."[2] Outwardly, she herself constantly struggled with illness, even while she was writing *The Interior Castle*.

As St. Teresa of Avila understood, to be human is to be both body and soul, so to live a spiritual life is not only about our interior attitudes and thoughts, but about our outward being and practices as well. We may tend to think of spirituality as simply remaining still with hands folded and eyes closed, but

---

1. St. Teresa of Avila, "The Sixth Mansion," ch. 1, in *The Interior Castle* (*The Mansions*), 1577, Christian Classics Ethereal Library, http://www.ccel.org/ccel/teresa/castle2.pdf, 3.
2. Ibid., 24.

that's just one possible expression of spiritual living among many other expressions that may be much more active. In the Gospels, we see Jesus at prayer, feeding the hungry, healing the sick, preaching and teaching, going up a mountain, walking on water, sleeping in a boat, sitting down at a well, in conversation with his followers and with those who opposed him, and expressing his life with God in many other active ways.

> **Stand at the crossroads, and look, and ask for the ancient paths, where the good way lies; and walk in it, and find rest for your souls (Jeremiah 6:16).**

In Scripture, walking is often used as a metaphor for spiritual living. The Law repeatedly reminded the people to walk in God's ways: "Therefore, keep the commandments of the LORD your God, by walking in his ways and by fearing him."[3] This is echoed by the prophets: "He has told you, O mortal, what is good; and what does the LORD require of you but to do justice, and to love kindness, and to walk humbly with your God?"[4] The letters to the early church are filled with references to walking in love,[5] walking by faith,[6] walking in truth,[7] walking in darkness or light[8]—all references not to the physical act of putting one foot in front of another, but to the spiritual life of faith.

One of the things I love about this metaphor of walking is that it's drawn from everyday life. Walking is not like running the Boston Marathon, or swimming across the English Channel, or climbing Mount Everest, or performing some other great feat. I walk to the grocery store, I walk for fitness and to visit a friend, I walk outside to enjoy nature. Walking is something ordinary that I can do at any time.

---

3. Deuteronomy 8:6; cf. 10:12; 11:22; 13:5; 19:9; 26:17; 28:9; 30:16.
4. Micah 6:8; cf. Isaiah 30:21; 65:2; Jeremiah 7:23-24.
5. Romans 14:15.
6. 2 Corinthians 5:7.
7. 2 John 1:4; 3 John 1:4.
8. 1 John 1:6-7; 2:11.

And yet, as Arthur Paul Boers points out, walking is also "an act of dissent; it is countercultural."[9] In North America, the automobile is still the preferred mode of transportation for many. In the city where I live, the installation of more bike lanes has been the cause of some controversy. Most drive to school, work, or church. Even I usually drive the

> *Journal Prompt*
>
> **What place does walking have in your life? When did you last go for a walk? Describe your experience.**

three minutes from home to church instead of walking—it's ten times faster, I have too much to carry, I need to go across town later anyway, I'm not wearing the right shoes, I have to pick up someone else, it's raining. As a child of my culture, I always seem to have a reason to drive instead of walk, to go faster instead of slower. So for me, walking is both an ordinary, everyday activity and yet challenges me as countercultural.

So too walking as metaphor for spiritual living. The spiritual life is something we can practice any day. I can take it one step at a time, not looking too far back or too far forward, focusing on the present moment. I can slow down. I can become quiet before God. I can pray. I can read Scripture. Just like walking down my street, these are ordinary things that I can do without any special training or skill. And yet they also go against the grain of my culture that tells me to do more and do it faster, a culture that values speaking up instead of being quiet, that sees prayer as unnecessary and Scripture as out of date. As a countercultural activity, walking is an apt metaphor for living a life of faith.

But can walking also be a spiritual practice in its own right? Is it more than a healthy alternative to driving? More than good physical exercise? Can it be more than a metaphor for spiritual living?

---

9. Arthur Paul Boers, *The Way Is Made by Walking* (Downers Grove: IVP Books, 2007), 164.

Walking with Scripture

When I was a teenager, I volunteered at a local hospital—watering plants, helping to deliver food trays, bringing magazines to patients, and generally making myself useful. I would sometimes take the bus to and from my weekly assignment, but most often I would walk home, happy to leave behind the close, overly warm air of the hospital. In the pocket of my coat I carried a small New Testament, the *New American Standard Bible*, and as I walked I would pull it out to read the letter of 1 John.

"What was from the beginning" (I would look up to cross the street and repeat the phrase to myself); "what we have heard, what we have seen with our eyes" (again repeating the phrase and looking up to see where I was going); "what we have looked at and touched with our hands, concerning the Word of Life" (again looking up and looking down as needed). As I walked week after week, I read and memorized the entire book to the last verse: "Little children, guard yourselves from idols."

As I walked even in wind and damp weather, fingering the pages over and over, the 1 John part of my little New Testament became noticeably worn compared to the rest of the book. How appropriate to be walking along as I repeated to myself, "By this we know that we are in Him: the one who says he abides in Him ought himself to walk in the same manner as He walked." The words of Scripture became part of the rhythm of my steps, "See how great a love the Father has bestowed on us," and part of the rhythm of my heart, "that we would be called children of God; and *such* we are."

Back then, I didn't think of my walking and reading as a spiritual discipline. Reading and memorizing Scripture was simply a way of having some company on my walk home. On days when I took the bus, my Bible stayed in my pocket. Maybe because the bus was usually crowded and standing room only. Maybe because I was surrounded by other people and didn't feel the same freedom to say the words aloud. For whatever reason, clearly it was the walk and being outdoors that made the difference.

That makes good sense to me since Scripture is full of the outdoors. The psalmists refer often to the natural world of sea and sky, earth and mountains, birds and animals. In the words of the prophet Isaiah, the mountains and hills sing and the trees clap their hands.[10] Jesus illustrated his teaching with lilies, birds, sowing seeds, wheat, and weeds. He walked everywhere, walked up mountains, even walked on water. Although I walked along city streets, I could see birds, trees, clouds in the sky, and mountains in the distance. I too could appreciate God's creation as the psalmists did. My walk with Scripture became an occasion for praise, prayer, and spiritual growth.

Prayer-walking

While on sabbatical from his rural congregation, S. Roy Kaufman says that he took a day-long walk outdoors every week, and when he returned to his church, he invited anyone in the congregation to join him for several monthly prayer walks of three to four hours each. The intention was to walk the neighborhood of the church to experience the natural world, to pray for members of the church at different points near their homes, and to learn more about their community. The small group of prayer walkers began each walk with Scripture and prayer. They walked, some in silence and some in conversation, pausing to pray for members by name. They learned more about one another and more about their surroundings. "Churches are often one-dimensional in the exercise of spiritual disciplines," notes Kaufman. "The prayer walk provided an alternative spiritual discipline for those uncomfortable in conventional prayer meeting settings."[11]

---

10. Isaiah 55:12.
11. S. Roy Kaufman, "The Anatomy of a Rural Church" in *The Mennonite* (September 2011), 18.

Besides my solo Scripture-walking and this kind of group prayer-walk, another form of prayer-walking is the labyrinth. Sometimes mistaken for a maze, a labyrinth is actually a single circular path for meditation and prayer that leads to and from its center. Those who walk the labyrinth do so at their own pace, pausing for prayer and silent reflection at any point along the way, allowing others who are moving more quickly or coming in the opposite direction to pass them, and moving past others who may be going more slowly. Walking a labyrinth is a form of personal prayer that can also be done with others.

In medieval Europe, many labyrinths were built as part of cathedrals and churches, and today there are labyrinths in North America too, some outdoors, some indoors, some permanent structures or painted on parking lots. Some say the labyrinth is symbolic of longer pilgrimages like England's Pilgrim's Way to Canterbury Cathedral, or Spain's 500-mile Camino de Santiago. On pilgrimage, the point is not simply to arrive at your destination; the journey on the way is just as important. So too with the labyrinth, the point is not simply to arrive at the center or to get there and back as quickly as possible; the journey of meditation and prayer along the way is key. I find that even the half hour or so spent walking the labyrinth can be a sort of pilgrimage, a sacred journey of communion with God.

Most days, though, when I go for a walk, I don't go in search of a labyrinth; instead, I simply start at my own front door. I no longer carry a New Testament in my pocket, but I sometimes

---

In his guide to prayer-walking, Linus Mundy proposes five movements:

(1) **Retreat: physically get away from house or office or wherever you normally spend your time.**

(2) **Rethink: consider the world around you.**

(3) **Remember: ponder your life to this point.**

(4) **Repent: be willing to make positive changes.**

(5) **Repeat: walk often.**

The Complete Guide to Prayer-Walking (New York: Crossroad, 1997), 40.

choose a verse for company as I walk, and I always have a lot
to pray about. I try to alternate walking at a more normal pace
with walking more briskly, which they say improves muscle
tone, protects the heart, gets more blood to the brain, and
lifts the spirit. I like not having to drive somewhere else to get
started, and if I stop at the produce store along the way, I also
save myself an extra trip for groceries. So is my walk spiritual
practice or physical exercise? An alternate form of transportation? Good psychology or good ecology? I suppose it's all of
those things at once.

That doesn't make it any less spiritual than sitting in quiet
reflection in the church sanctuary, or praying with head bowed
and eyes closed. As we walk, we can pray with eyes wide open
and marvel at God's creation. We can hold a verse of Scripture
in our mind and heart even as we wait for a green light or bend
to smell a flower. Taking a prayer-walk is simply a different form
of spiritual practice, engaging both body and soul, a reflection
of what it means for us to be people of "the Way,"[12] always on
the move with God who goes with us.

Sacred pause: walk the talk

On the traffic station the other day, the announcer said, "Spend
less time getting where you're going, and more time being where
you want to be." When I'm on my way to an appointment and
feel pressed for time, that's exactly why I listen to that station.
If there's a car stalled on the bridge or if construction is backing up traffic, I'd rather do what I can to avoid them, and yes,
exactly, spend less time getting where I'm going and more time
being where I want to be.

But what's best for driving doesn't apply to walking as
spiritual practice. If anything, I'd say that walking as spiritual
practice means spending more time getting where I'm going, if

---

12. Acts 9:2; 19:9, 23; 22:4; 24:14, 22.

only to end up back at home. It's not about getting to some new and exciting destination, but being on the journey with God.

To try this for yourself, choose one or more of the options listed here. If you're short on time or physical energy, start with a walk of just a few minutes and build up to something more as you are able. For the greatest benefit, you might want to walk every day. But be mindful of your own physical condition and don't overdo it. It's not a competition, even with yourself.

Getting sidetracked

Don't worry if you get sidetracked when you're out for a walk. It's not any less spiritual if you get interrupted. So say hello to passersby. Stop to talk to a neighbor. Realize that walking with a young child may mean stopping to examine a caterpillar or collect rocks. One woman always walks with a plastic bag so she can pick up any trash along the way.

(1) Take a short walk. Even a few minutes to get out of the office or to walk through your own backyard can be a refreshing change. Read Luke 24:13-16. What things keep you from recognizing Jesus in your life?

(2) Go for a nature walk in a nearby park. Read Psalm 24 before you head out the door. What difference does it make to think of the whole earth and everything in it as the Lord's? End your walk by reading Matthew 6:25-34. "So do not worry about tomorrow, for tomorrow will bring worries of its own. Today's trouble is enough for today."[13]

(3) Plan a prayer walk around your neighborhood. Think about where you would stop along the way. Do you know your neighbors? Is there a school nearby? A community center? A library? A church? Storefronts? Read Matthew 22:34-40 before you start. Reflect on what it means to love your neighbor and how you might pray for them.

(4) Go for a longer hike. Pack a sandwich and a piece of fruit and a bottle of water. Dress in layers. Stash your Bible

---

13. Matthew 6:34.

and journal in your backpack. Read Isaiah 43:1-4 before you go. Consider reading Psalms 120–134 at different points along the way, since these were psalms written for pilgrims traveling to the temple in Jerusalem. They offer words of comfort and encouragement for people on a journey. "Happy is everyone who fears the LORD, who walks in his ways."[14]

(5) If you are interested in walking a labyrinth, check out the World-Wide Labyrinth Locator at http://labyrinthlocator.com/. Some are public, some private, some portable and available for borrowing. As you walk, you may wish to pray the Lord's Prayer. Or pray for personal concerns on your way to the center, pause to give thanks, then pray for others as you make your way back out. Ask God to guide your prayer time.

---

14. Psalm 128:1.

7

Being Alone without Being Lonely

I commune with my heart in the night;
I meditate and search my spirit. . . .
Psalm 77:6

What place does solitude have in your life? When William Deresiewicz posed this question to his English students at Yale University, he was surprised at their answers. One student confessed to being "freaked out" by solitude. Another asked, "Why would anyone ever want to be alone? What can you get out of being alone that you can't get by being with someone else?"

For these students so used to being connected by text, Facebook, and Twitter, the thought of some quality time alone was quite foreign. Technology helped them communicate more and faster, but Deresiewicz wondered if technology was also interfering with their ability to be alone without feeling lonely. In our hyper-connected world, are we losing a "capacity for solitude," and does that matter?

Deresiewicz argues that it does matter, that "no real excellence, personal or social, artistic, philosophical, scientific or moral, can arise without solitude."[1] Certainly, solitude allows time for sustained reading and thinking, for the kind of

---

1. William Deresiewicz, "The End of Solitude" in *The Chronicle of Higher Education*, Washington, D.C., January 30, 2009, http://chronicle.com/article/The-End-of-Solitude/3708, and a full interview by Nora Hill for CBC, February 19, 2009, http://www.cbc.ca/spark/full-interviews/2009/02/19/full-interview-william-deresiewicz-on-the-end-of-solitude/.

creativity that's part of excellence. There are many other benefits, like the space and time to develop our own goals and sense
of purpose; time for reflection and prayer; reading Scripture,
journaling, and other spiritual practices; for discovering who
we are apart from our family, friends, and other people.

Solitude can be transformative as we "derole,"[2] taking a step
back from our many roles and responsibilities to gain new perspective and return to them with new vision and new energy.
What's more, becoming absorbed in a solitary pursuit—whether
music or art or snowboarding—can be just plain fun! As
Deresiewicz tried to tell his students, there is much to be gained
by spending time alone that you can't get by constantly being
with others.

Journal Prompt

**When was the last time you were
alone? Was it solitude or loneliness?
How did it make you feel?**

Loneliness from the inside out

From the beginning, we were created for companionship: "The
LORD God said, 'It is not good that the man should be alone,'"[3]
so it's no wonder that we might experience the absence of others
as loneliness. The great American evangelist Billy Graham once
said that loneliness is one of the most important issues facing
humankind.[4] That's not only a religious perspective; political
speech writer Peggy Noonan identifies loneliness as the biggest
problem facing any modern industrial society, and that's why
speeches from political leaders are important, she says, because
they help to ease the sense of isolation.[5]

2. Ross Kingham, *Surprises of the Spirit* (Australia: Barnabas Communications,
1991), 32.
3. Genesis 2:18.
4. http://www.billygraham.org/articlepage.asp?articleid=7646 is one version of
his classic sermon on loneliness.
5. Peggy Noonan, *What I Saw at the Revolution* (New York: Random House,
1990), 69.

Loneliness is such a common human experience that most people reading this book will have felt lonely at one time or another. It's such a personal experience that you can feel lonely even when you're with other people. Even while apparently surrounded by others, the psalmist still felt alone: "Look on my right hand and see—there is no one who takes notice of me; no refuge remains to me; no one cares for me."[6]

Whatever may be going on around us, loneliness is more about our inward state. It's a sense of isolation, separation, alienation from the inside out that can occur any time and anywhere.

Hannah Whitall Smith understood that well. She was a devout Christian in the nineteenth century, perhaps most well known for her book *The Christian's Secret of a Happy Life*. When a single friend wrote a letter to Hannah about being lonely, Hannah wrote back,

> The loneliness you speak of, I know. For do not think that it is confined to unmarried people. It is just as real in lives that have plenty of human ties, husbands, and children and friends. I believe it is inseparable from humanity. I believe God has ordained it in the very nature of things by creating us for Himself alone. Therefore nothing but God can satisfy it. . . . it is a God-given blessing meant only to drive you to himself.[7]

Even if we do all the "right" things—use the right toothpaste, develop a hobby, join a club or a church, form good friendships, marry, and have children and grandchildren—we'll still be lonely at times.

But in spiritual terms, with Hannah Whitall Smith, we might also say blessed are the lonely—not because it's good

6. Psalm 142:4.
7. Quaker Letters. A letter to Miss Priscilla Mounsey, Germantown, PA, January 18, 1882.

to feel bad, but because loneliness can function as a spiritual spur toward God. Blessed are the lonely who are able to look beyond their loneliness. Blessed are the lonely who realize their own need and turn to God. Blessed are the lonely who develop a capacity for solitude.

> For God alone my soul waits
>   in silence;
> from him comes my salvation.
> He alone is my rock and my
>   salvation, my fortress;
> I shall never be shaken (Psalm 62:1-2).

In search of solitude

In the book of Genesis, Jacob spent a night alone before continuing on his journey to meet his estranged brother, Esau. That night, Jacob wrestled with his own thoughts, he wrestled with an angel of God, and he was changed forever, receiving the new name of Israel and left with a limp to remind him of his encounter with God.[8] In Exodus Moses was alone tending his father-in-law's sheep when he saw a bush as if it were on fire, but when he drew closer for a better look, God spoke to him and called him to lead his people out of Egypt.[9]

As Jesus began his public ministry, he also spent time alone before beginning his mission among his people:

> In the morning, while it was still very dark, he got up and went out to a deserted place, and there he prayed. And Simon and his companions hunted for him.
>
> When they found him, they said to him, "Everyone is searching for you."
>
> He answered, "Let us go on to the neighboring towns, so that I may proclaim the message there also; for that is what I came out to do."
>
> And he went throughout Galilee, proclaiming the message in their synagogues and casting out demons.[10]

8. Genesis 32:24-31.
9. Exodus 3:1-10.
10. Mark 1:35-39.

As Jesus drew his earthly ministry to an end, he again spent time alone, praying in the Garden of Gethsemane on the night of his arrest[11] and dying alone on the cross.[12]

Jesus' entire ministry is characterized by a deliberate rhythm of time with others and time alone. Before calling his twelve disciples, he spent an entire night in prayer, alone on a mountain.[13] After the death of John the Baptist, Jesus withdrew to a place where he could be alone.[14] After teaching the crowds all day and multiplying bread and fish enough to feed them all, Jesus sent his disciples off to the next town by boat, while he stayed behind for a time of solitude and prayer.[15] After an intense time of teaching the crowds, Jesus went to the region of Tyre to be alone.[16] He encouraged his disciples also to take some time away by themselves, for they were so busy that they barely had enough time to eat.[17]

Jesus was so at home with solitude that he seemed most lonely when he was with other people. When he prayed alone on the night of his arrest, his disciples were actually with him nearby, but they were apparently unaware of his distress and even fell asleep while he prayed in agony. Jesus' remark afterward to Simon Peter is a measure of his loneliness, "So, could you not stay awake with me one hour?"[18]

On the cross, when Jesus felt abandoned even by God—"my God, my God, why have you forsaken me?"[19]—his loneliness was not relieved by the others who were crucified with him or by the bystanders that heard him cry out. While physically

---

11. Matthew 26:36ff.
12. Matthew 27:46.
13. Luke 6:12-16.
14. Matthew 14:13.
15. Mark 6:45-46.
16. Mark 7:24.
17. Mark 6:31-32.
18. Matthew 26:40.
19. Mark 15:34.

Never really alone

Not long before his arrest, Jesus said to his disciples, "The hour is coming, indeed it has come, when you will be scattered, each one to his home, and you will leave me alone. Yet I am not alone because the Father is with me" (John 16:32).

The apostle Paul describes a similar experience when he was arrested and put on trial in Rome: "At my first defense no one came to my support, but all deserted me. . . . But the Lord stood by me and gave me strength" (2 Timothy 4:16-17).

Though others may have deserted them, both Jesus and Paul were confident of God's presence and power in their lives. They were never really alone, because God was with them. For us too, God's faithful presence means that even when we may feel the most lonely, we are never really alone.

surrounded by others, he was keenly aware of how they misunderstood and rejected him, leaving him alone in his suffering.

In contrast, Jesus' experience of being physically by himself, in solitude with God alone, was a much more positive experience. In solitude, he was able to prepare for his mission, to pray and discern God's will, to gather vision and strength for his ministry. Solitude gave him the space to mourn the death of John the Baptist before going on with his own ministry. Solitude was his place to pray, to rest, and to be refreshed.

Solitude interrupted

According to the gospel accounts, however, for Jesus, solitude was often solitude interrupted. When he heard that John the Baptist had been killed by Herod, Jesus tried to withdraw to a quiet place by boat, but by the time he reached the shore, a great crowd had already gathered, and "he had compassion for them and cured their sick."[20]

After an intense time of teaching the crowds and answering the Pharisees and scribes who opposed him, Jesus went to Tyre some distance away, hoping to spend time alone, but even

---

20. Matthew 14:14.

there he attracted attention. No sooner had he arrived when a woman approached him with a plea to heal her daughter from an evil spirit. Once again, Jesus' solitude was interrupted, and once again he had compassion on the woman and her daughter, and the little girl was set free.[21]

Each time Jesus was interrupted, he responded with compassion instead of complaint, with a heart for the needs of others in spite of his own needs. He set aside his own need for rest to help a woman and her daughter. He set aside his own mourning for John the Baptist and spent the day instead healing the sick.

As the day drew to a close, when Jesus and his disciples were all tired, his disciples also wanted some time alone and suggested sending the crowd away. But Jesus insisted that they should feed the crowd first, and it was only much later that he and his disciples were finally able to be alone.[22]

How would you and I have responded in the same situation? When life doesn't turn out the way we've planned, do we respond with compassion for others? When we're interrupted, do we respond accordingly and come back to our own plans later? What place does discernment have here? Are we to receive all interruptions as divine appointments and signs of God's grace? Or are there times when we need to stay the course, draw a firm boundary, and ignore interruptions?

After all, even Jesus did not heal all the sick, or cure all the lame, or raise all the dead. So humanly speaking there were certainly some limits to his ministry. But I also notice that Jesus was not overly concerned with drawing boundaries, not overly concerned with reserving time for himself alone, but able to respond to others with generosity and compassion. As he would later make the ultimate sacrifice by giving up his life on the cross, he gave sacrificially of his time and energy throughout his life.

---

21. Mark 7:24-30.
22. Matthew 14:13-23.

A student once asked to interview me on the risk of burn-out among pastors, and while I was glad to talk with him and appreciated his desire to be well prepared for ministry, it seemed to me that he was a bit too concerned about guarding time for himself. For all the legitimate concerns about stress and burnout in ministry and in life—and I do believe we need to be proactive and pay attention to these things—I also wonder whether it's possible to be too careful, to draw our boundaries too tightly and so miss out on showing compassion and allowing God's grace and power to be revealed in us.

You and I are only human with limited time and energy. You and I are not Jesus. But just as we ask ourselves what place solitude has in our lives, we might also ask what place is there for sacrifice? What might be a healthy rhythm of time with others and time alone, of engagement and solitude, of active ministry and spiritual practice, of time on and time out? Can we appreciate and take time for solitude, and appreciate and take time for solitude interrupted as well?

Sacred pause: practice solitude

(1) If you are often alone, set aside some deliberate time to be alone with God. How might that be different from simply being by yourself? Turn off your cell phone, your laptop, your television, your MP3 player, and any other gadgets. Read Scripture. Pray. Simply rest in God's presence.

(2) If life is busy for you, take advantage of moments of solitude throughout the day, however small or infrequent: standing in line at the library, reclining in the dentist chair, waiting to pick up your son or daughter from soccer practice or music lessons. Close your eyes; take a deep breath and let it out slowly. Spend this moment alone with God. Suspend your busy thoughts, and simply rest in God's presence. If you have a pressing concern, imagine it as an object that you can hold in your hands; feel its weight; imagine its shape, color, and texture; and

then release it to God. If you are interrupted, attend to the demands of daily life as needed, confident of God's power at work in you. Return to solitude when you can.

(3) If you are rarely alone, plan to spend some time by yourself this week—whether it be a few moments, an hour, a morning, an afternoon, a day. Give yourself permission to disconnect from your family and social network. Turn off your cell phone, your laptop, your television, your MP3 player, and any other gadgets. Use this time for solitude as spiritual practice. Go for a long walk, run, or bike ride, read, pray, think, cook a meal from scratch, lift weights, do a jigsaw puzzle—but plan to do it alone. If you are interrupted, ask for God's blessing and patience, and practice compassion. Then return to your time alone when you are able.

8

Valuing Relationships

Trust in him at all times, O people;
pour out your heart before him;
God is a refuge for us.
Psalm 62:8

On most retreats, we remove ourselves from our usual surroundings and relationships, leaving family and others
behind. We leave behind the expectations of the everyday for
a new set of expectations, whether solitude or prayer, a long
walk in the woods, mulling over a decision, or simply taking a
break to rest and catch up on sleep. But while we may think of a
retreat primarily in terms of getting away from it all, including
our relationships, that time away can also affect our relationships in a powerful way.

For some, the old saying "absence makes the heart grow
fonder" proves to be true as they return from retreat with a
renewed appreciation for family, and their family joyfully welcomes them back. For some, time on retreat is a time for reevaluating relationships, and they return determined to make
some changes in the way they relate to family members or
colleagues. Others may find healing for difficult relationships,
letting go of the pain, learning to forgive, setting boundaries
that help them to move forward with their lives.

A spiritual practice of valuing our relationships may also
mean taking time for reevaluating, for finding healing, for coming to a renewed appreciation for family, friends, and others

who are part of our lives. It may mean taking time for spiritual friendship, spiritual direction, or meeting with a mentor. Far from being isolating or antirelationship in any way, the flip side of solitude is valuing relationships.

Enough said?

Those who are eager to get to the practical application might wonder why anything more needs to be said. Of course relationships are important. God created us in and for community: "Then God said, 'Let us make humankind in our image, according to our likeness. . . .' So God created humankind in his image, in the image of God he created them; male and female he created them."[1] The psalmist adds, "How very good and pleasant it is when kindred live together in unity!"[2] From Scripture and from our own experience, we know that relationships are important.

> Two are better than one,
> because they have a good reward
>   for their toil.
> For if they fall, one will lift up
>   the other;
> but woe to one who is alone
>   and falls
> and does not have another to help
> (Ecclesiastes 4:9-10).

Yet everywhere I look there are so many broken relationships. In the news today, another celebrity couple is getting a divorce; teachers are involved in an ongoing dispute with the government; there are broken relationships on a national and international scale.

It's not only what I see in the news. Broken relationships are part of my life too. Divorce and remarriage are part of my own family and church family. I'm all too familiar with personal and work-related disagreements, even theological disagreements that have led to broken relationships. I struggle to keep in touch with extended family and friends, not wanting to let

---

1. Genesis 1:26-27.
2. Psalm 133:1.

geographical distance or limited time or personality differences destroy our connection. Relationships can be hard work, but they're also vital for our personal and spiritual health.

For better, for worse

The book of Romans is a powerful statement of faith that covers everything from how we relate to God to how we relate to ourselves to how we relate to one another. It takes us from sin to salvation, from judgment to justification. With its broad scope and somewhat technical language, the book of Romans may seem less like a personal letter and more like a theological textbook. And yet chapter 16, the last chapter of the book, is devoted to greetings with a long list of personal names.

Real church, real relationship

For the apostle Paul, the church was a key place for relationship. He once described the church as a body, where all the members are related and work together, just as all the parts of the body are related and work together (1 Corinthians 12). At its best, the church is a place and people of worship, who care for one another and support one another, who work together and continually expand their body to include others. For Paul, there was no such thing as an individual believer, for all who believed in Christ needed to follow him, and all who followed him were joined together in one body by his Spirit.

That's why church is important—not as a religious institution or something to go to every Sunday; not because it's perfect because it's not; not because you won't ever get hurt because you quite likely will. Real churches have real problems and blind spots, and wherever there are people there is also brokenness. But real church also means real relationship, with God and with others.

So if you're already an active part of a church, then keep it real and carry on. If you've become lukewarm, ask yourself what would it take to change your attitude. If you're reluctant to give church a try because you've been hurt by the church or have never gone, take some time to ask around, do some research, go with a friend, or be brave and go alone. Think of the time of worship together as a sacred pause. Allow the music, prayers, and silence to carry you into God's presence.

In the second century, a former bishop of the church named Marcion decided to omit this last chapter from his copy of the book of Romans. The long list of names seemed out of place in what otherwise appeared to be a great statement of faith, so he simply took it out. Today we might be tempted to do the same—to skip over the long list of ancient names that are unfamiliar to us, that are hard to read, hard to pronounce, hard to listen to. But instead of dismissing these personal greetings, we need to see them in light of the rest of the letter.

The first fifteen chapters of Romans are like a sermon that talks about what Christians believe and how they should live out their beliefs. Then chapter 16 is the sermon illustrated in the lives of real people and in their real relationships. The book of Romans is not really complete without the final chapter, because a statement of faith is not really complete until it is lived out by real people in the real world.

The apostle Paul valued each of these relationships enough to include them in his letter: those with Greek names like Phoebe and Apelles that indicated their Greek background; those with Jewish names like Aquila and Mary that indicated their Jewish background. Priscilla and Aquila were a married couple who owned a tentmaking business; Persis and Philologus were common slave names; Tryphaena and Tryphosa may have been twin sisters; the household of Aristobulus and the household of Narcissus likely included parents, grandparents, aunts, uncles, brothers, sisters, children, any single people, any widows, any servants. Over and over again, throughout this long and diverse list of names, Paul greets each one warmly and acknowledges them "in the Lord."[3] At the same time, the apostle Paul also had his share of difficult relationships. In his ministry of preaching the gospel and planting churches, he met with opposition from both religious and civil authorities. Paul and Barnabas

---

3. Romans 16:1-15.

were ejected from the city of Pisidian Antioch and had to flee for safety from the city of Iconium. Paul was stoned in Lystra, arrested along with Silas and put into jail in Philippi. Finally he was arrested in Jerusalem and sent to Rome.[4]

At times, Paul experienced strained relationships even with his colleagues. He publicly criticized Peter for first accepting Gentiles into the church and then refusing to eat with them.[5] He had an even more serious dispute with Barnabas, who had been one of his first supporters and had worked closely with him planting churches.

When the two men planned to revisit each city to see how the believers were doing, Barnabas wanted John Mark to accompany them, but Paul refused. Mark had not followed through on an earlier assignment, and Paul was not yet ready to have him back as a traveling companion and coworker. The disagreement between Barnabas and Paul became so sharp that they parted ways with Barnabas and Mark going in one direction and Paul and Silas in another.[6]

There's no clear record that Paul ever mended his relationship with Barnabas and Mark, but perhaps all three were reconciled at some point, for toward the end of his life Paul would write to Timothy, "Get Mark and bring him with you, for he is useful in my ministry."[7] Perhaps by that time Mark had changed, grown up, and learned to follow through on his commitments. And so perhaps Paul had changed as well, able to forgive and forget the past and to accept Mark for what he could contribute.

In personality and temperament, Paul was fiercely independent, headstrong, outspoken. I can imagine that Barnabas and others had difficulty working with him on more than one occasion. His relationships were sometimes for better as he

4. Acts 13–28.
5. Galatians 2:11-14.
6. Acts 15:36-41.
7. 2 Timothy 4:11.

acknowledged his partners in the gospel, and sometimes for worse when he came into conflict with them. Relationships were apparently hard work for him, too. But at least he never took them for granted. He was able to acknowledge them, to be authentic even if it meant disagreement, not getting stuck in the past but able to grow and change.

Getting personal

One year I decided to try praying for every member of our church on their birthday, and also phoning or sending them an email or card. It was part of my ministry of prayer, and yet for me it was also a sacred pause, a step away from other daily ministry tasks to reflect and pray for each person. Looking back, I realize that it had been an overly ambitious goal, as I spent much of the year behind and didn't manage to go back and complete the whole church list until well into January of the following year.

But it was also a precious time of blessing others. Some responded with prayers of their own. Some said they felt special. Others shared something that they were going through personally or in their family that made prayer especially timely for them. I didn't hear back from everyone—I didn't expect that I would—but I wanted to acknowledge and pray for each one regardless of the response, and it proved to be a valuable spiritual discipline.

I have also been on the receiving end as others have blessed me. For my birthday one year, I was surprised to hear on my voice mail a chorus of voices singing "Happy Birthday." Touched that a mother and her four children had taken a moment in their busy family life to wish me a happy birthday, I saved their voice mail for months afterward. Another time I received in the regular mail a handwritten note from a friend. It wasn't her annual Christmas card, it wasn't for my birthday, but a note "just because" to recognize our friendship over the years. "I'm so thankful for all my friends," she wrote, "that I'm sending you a note to let you know."

Unfortunately, not all of my interactions are so positive. I like to think I get along with everyone, but one time my husband and I lived in an apartment building with a neighbor who had difficulty with us. We had our bathroom fan on too long. He could hear our footsteps even on our carpeted floors. He complained about us to the management. The manager told us, "Don't worry about it. You have to live. It's normal to hear your neighbors when you live in a wood-frame building. Some people can't get used to that." Still, we tried to walk more quietly. We switched off the bathroom fan as soon as we could. We tried to greet our neighbor pleasantly whenever we saw him. Sadly, nothing seemed to help, and I think he was relieved when we eventually moved away.

> **Do not repay anyone evil for evil, but take thought for what is noble in the sight of all. If it is possible, so far as it depends on you, live peaceably with all (Romans 12:17-18).**

Perhaps the manager was right that some people aren't well-suited to apartment living, perhaps our neighbor was unwell as others suggested, but for whatever reason, our efforts to change our behavior just weren't enough to satisfy him. Our attempts at reconciliation failed. All I could do was to commit him to God and wish him well. I'm sorry that we weren't able to be on better terms with him, and wherever he may be today, I do hope that he has better neighbors.

Sacred pause: value your relationships

As you reflect on your own relationships, choose one or both of the following options:

(1) How might you pause to value your relationship(s), and offer a blessing to others? Will you pray for someone? Telephone, text, or write a note? Drop off some flowers? Meet for coffee? Give them a hug?

Don't simply add this to your already overcrowded to-do list as one more chore. It's not meant to be a burden. Instead, consider what might be refreshing for yourself and for the other person. If you're short on time, you might take just a moment to phone and leave a message of appreciation. Or if you have time, take a walk together or have a leisurely coffee.

Journal Prompt

List three people who have contributed to who you are today, and offer a prayer of thanks for each one.

Whatever you choose doesn't need to take a lot of time, as long as it's real and from the heart.

(2) Do you have a relationship that needs mending? Do you need to offer an apology or be able to accept one? Or is some other way of making peace required? Take a deep breath, gather your thoughts, offer another prayer, and focus. Then go ahead and make that apology or do whatever is necessary to make things right.

If you're not sure what to do next, you may find it helpful to journal about your situation. Talk to God about it, or simply hold it before God in prayer. If even that is too difficult, then simply set it aside for now, and focus instead on relationships that you can appreciate. Even if you are not able to address your difficult relationship at this time, be assured that God is at work within you and between you. Let it go for now, resolve to come back to it later, and let God take it from here.

9

Giving

Offer right sacrifices,
and put your trust in the Lord.
Psalm 4:5

One day I answered a knock at our door and found my neighbor and his son on our doorstep. "I'm canvassing for the Diabetes Association," he said, "and I'm wondering if you would like to make a donation." That same week I received a letter from the university where I graduated years ago, also asking for a donation. My niece was selling tickets to raise funds for her figure skating. A boy from our neighborhood asked me to sponsor him in a walkathon to raise money for computers at his school. At the grocery store, I was met by Boy Scouts selling hotdogs to support their activities.

At church, it seemed like more of the same. Our finance committee had a notice in the bulletin about giving to our church budget. There was a fundraiser announcement to support the youth and a request for funds to help with disaster relief.

All of these church, community, and world needs were legitimate and important, and I contributed to many of them. But so many requests coming in the same week also made me feel like saying, "Time out!" My head was swimming from the constant pleas for money coming from every direction. I could well understand those who speak of "donor fatigue" and "donor frustration." It felt like Operation Overload.

The pleas for money from every quarter aren't any less now than they were during that one week. If anything, the need for funds in every area of good works has increased, and the requests keep coming. Is there no rest, no retreat from the responsibility to give and give and keep on giving?

I gave at the office

Today we might think of giving as just one more chore. But in Scripture, giving is not described as a chore at all. Instead, it was part of the Sabbath rest and celebration. When the Hebrew people gave their tithe, they were told to celebrate![1] In giving, they acknowledged God who provided for all their needs and enabled them to give. In giving, they honored God as the Lord of all. They were to give freely, confident that God would provide, not bound to their possessions but bound instead to their Lord.

Journal Prompt

Name three possessions that you value. Why are they important to you? Would you—could you—give them away? Why or why not?

In the Sermon on the Mount, Jesus is clear, "No one can serve two masters; for a slave will either hate the one and love the other, or be devoted to the one and despise the other. You cannot serve God and wealth."[2] As an example of faithful giving, Jesus points out a widow who puts two coins in the temple treasury; instead of bringing a tithe, she gives "everything she had, all she had to live on."[3] In a letter to the early church, the apostle Paul writes, "Each of you must give as you have made up your mind, not reluctantly or under compulsion, for God loves a cheerful giver. And God is able to provide you with every blessing in abundance, so that by always having enough of everything, you may share abundantly in every good work."[4]

1. Deuteronomy 14:22-26.
2. Matthew 6:24.
3. Mark 12:44.
4. 2 Corinthians 9:7-8.

Does all of that sound hopelessly idealistic? Unrealistic? As much as I want to admire the widow who gives all she has, I wonder why she's not more like the industrious woman of Proverbs 31 in handling her money more wisely. And why is nothing said about the social and structural issues of the widow's poverty that made her give too much while the wealthy and powerful gave too little? I wonder if those who gave in the Bible were always cheerful, always confident in God. Or did they sometimes give grudgingly or out of guilt? Or even refuse to give?

The prophets often addressed the social and structural issues of their day and had strong words for leaders who abused their power and kept others poor.[5] Just before Jesus points out the poor widow and her offering, he speaks out against the scribes who "devour widows' houses."[6] In the early church, Ananias and Sapphira sell a piece of property, and while they give some of the proceeds to the church, they pretend that they had given the entire amount.[7] Not everyone in Scripture gave freely and cheerfully in honor to God.

Take time to pray

If you feel overwhelmed by too many requests for money, gather up all the letters, flyers, and other information, and silently offer them up to God. Take time to pray: Lord, which of these many needs am I to support at this time? Which needs am I to leave to others? Guide me as I seek to be deliberate about giving.

And yet at its best, if giving is a sign of freedom from the things that weigh us down, if it springs from confidence in God's provision and out of a cheerful spirit, if giving is meant to be a celebration in honor of God's goodness, it sounds like the kind of personal renewal I'm looking for—time out from giving as a chore, and time to give in acts of justice and

---

5. Isaiah 3:13–4:1; cf. Amos 4:1-3.
6. Mark 12:40.
7. Acts 5:1-11.

celebration. Can we be cheerful and confident givers? Can we find rest from donor fatigue and place our trust in God?

Giving as spiritual practice

Since personal and household circumstances vary widely, I can't imagine finding a one-size-fits-all approach to cheerful giving. Some people are working hard just to make ends meet. Some have more money than they really need and put it toward travel or recreational properties or other things. Others are living on borrowed money, owing more than they actually have. Some have more dependents than others. Some are unemployed or employed only part time. Some are retired.

Our situations are all different and change at different points throughout our lives, so we will need to make our own uniquely different decisions time and time again. As you explore giving as spiritual practice, consider the following:

(1) *Recognize giving as a way of connecting with God.* There's a scene in *Jesus Christ Superstar* where Jesus is surrounded by lepers asking, begging, pleading for him to touch them and make them well. They press in on him, reach for him, almost engulf him with their cries and their urgent pleas for healing. When I think of giving like that, I feel overwhelmed by all the pleas for help. But when I think of giving as spiritual practice, I shift my focus from how overwhelmed I feel to how much I need to listen for God's voice. Instead of being pulled every which way, engulfed by the many requests, I realize that it's not all up to me. Instead, I can place my trust in God, the Creator and Lord of All.

Early in our married life, my husband and I decided that we would give away 10 percent of whatever we earned. As we were both students, that tithe didn't amount to a lot, but for us it was still an act of trust. Could we make enough at our summer jobs to study full time? How would we pay for rent and food and tuition and books, let alone tithe? How far could we stretch our shoestring budget? Yet we continued to tithe, and during those lean years, we learned that it wasn't all about us. As a spiritual practice, giving taught us to place our trust in God.

(2) *Acknowledge that everything belongs to God.* It's easy to think and speak in terms of "my" house, "my" car, "my" money. My name might be on the mortgage papers or the rental agreement, I might have a license for the car, I deposit the money in a bank account with my name on it. But as the Source and Sustainer of all things, God is really the "owner" of all that we have—not 10 percent, but 100 percent. "For every wild animal of the forest is mine, the cattle on a thousand hills. I know all the birds of the air, and all that moves in the field is mine. If I were hungry, I would not tell you, for the world and all that is in it is mine."[8]

If everything already belongs to God, then whatever I can give is really minuscule. God really has no need of my small offering, but

> *More than tithing*
>
> **Ten percent is a rather arbitrary amount. Although Scripture speaks of tithing, there are references also to "your burnt offerings and your sacrifices, your tithes and your donations, your votive gifts, your freewill offerings, and the firstlings of your herds and flocks" (Deuteronomy 12:6). Jesus' commendation of the widow who gives everything is further evidence that giving was not meant to be limited to 10 percent. Theologian Reinhold Niebuhr suggests proportionate giving, beginning with a tithe as an "economic floor."**
> **Cited in Elizabeth O'Connor, *Letters to Scattered Pilgrims* (San Francisco: Harper & Row, 1979), 6–7.**

I need to give it to remind myself. I don't need to hold on to "my" money so tightly because it belongs to God. I can go out of my way to pick up someone for Bible study because I'm driving God's car. "My" house can be a place of hospitality because it's God's house. A spirit of giving applies to what I give away, and a spirit of giving also applies to how I use the things I keep, because everything belongs to God.

---

8. Psalm 50:10-12.

(3) *Realize that giving means more than tangible things like money or possessions.* As Jesus says, "Woe to you, scribes and Pharisees, hypocrites! For you tithe mint, dill, and cummin, and have neglected the weightier matters of the law: justice and mercy and faith. It is these you ought to have practiced without neglecting the others."[9] Here Jesus seems to assume a tithe, but even that was nothing in comparison to justice, mercy, and faith. Tithing to the letter of the law was not complete unless these qualities were practiced as well.

> **What good is it, my brothers and sisters, if you say you have faith but do not have works? Can faith save you? If a brother or sister is naked and lacks daily food, and one of you says to them, "Go in peace; keep warm and eat your fill," and yet you do not supply their bodily needs, what is the good of that? (James 2:14-16).**

The prophet Isaiah had strong words for the rich: "What do you mean by crushing my people, by grinding the face of the poor? says the LORD GOD of hosts."[10] The prophet Micah asked, "and what does the LORD require of you but to do justice, and to love kindness, and to walk humbly with your God?"[11] We also need to ask, Do I pay workers fairly? Do I seek justice for those who are oppressed? Do I have mercy for the ragged man on the street asking for change? Can I show mercy to the poor driver who's trying to merge onto a busy highway? Do I have faith in God's provision for my life? If our giving is to be genuine, we need to ask such questions of justice, mercy, and faith.

(4) *Give and be free.* Much has been written about North American excess, how we consume far more than our share of the earth's resources, how we seem to be driven by a desire for more and more.[12] In many ways, our culture of consumerism

---

9. Matthew 23:23.
10. Isaiah 3:15.
11. Micah 6:8.
12. Albert Y. Hsu, *The Suburban Christian: Finding Spiritual Vitality in the Land of Plenty* (Downers Grove: IVP Books, 2006).

embodies this warning from Scripture: "Those who want to be rich fall into temptation and are trapped by many senseless and harmful desires that plunge people into ruin and destruction. For the love of money is a root of all kinds of evil, and in their eagerness to be rich some have wandered away from the faith and pierced themselves with many pains."[13]

In contrast, giving is a way of saying no to this culture of consumerism, a way of treading more lightly on the earth, and not being weighed down by excess baggage. Last month I cleaned out our closets and basement storage room. I packed up all the clothes we no longer wear, some books and magazines we were ready to give away, a lamp we don't use, and other miscellaneous household items. In all, I gathered up enough to fill four large garbage bags, and it felt good to haul everything out to the curb to be picked up by a local charity.

I felt freer just giving away these items that I no longer used. How much more freeing to give in other ways: to buy a cup of coffee for the next person in line, to make a donation to a women's shelter, to give time to tutor a newcomer in English. As we give, we shift our focus from being preoccupied with our own lives to considering the needs of others, from accumulating more and more to using what we have in positive and life-giving ways. We can be free.

(5) *Celebrate!* In the Sermon on the Mount, Jesus speaks out against those who would "sound a trumpet" when they make their offering.[14] They liked to be seen and praised by others. So yes, they were celebrating, but they were celebrating their own gift instead of the Giver!

When friends recently bought a house, they chose to celebrate with a time of thanks and blessing for their new home. They wanted to dedicate it as a place of refreshment, a place of hospitality, a place to reach out to others. As they envisioned

---

13. 1 Timothy 6:9-10.
14. Matthew 6:1-4.

how they would give their home in service, they wanted to celebrate God who had given it to them. So they invited a few friends to share together with Scripture and prayer, stories, laughter, refreshments. It was a celebration of God's goodness: "O LORD, I love the house in which you dwell, and the place where your glory abides."[15]

Sacred pause: celebrate giving

Giving as a spiritual practice connects us with God, who is the Creator and Sustainer of all things. It connects us with other people and other places as we look both within ourselves and without to the world around us.

Begin then by reflecting on all that God has given you—both materially and spiritually, the measure of health and abilities that God has given you. Reflect on the more immediate needs you are aware of, as well as wider social needs for compassion and justice. Then consider what you might offer without any thought of return. Giving is not some spiritual scheme for getting back more money or more blessings. As Paul quotes Jesus, "It is more blessed to give than to receive."[16] Giving is itself a blessing!

If you need some ideas, read through the list that follows, but don't limit yourself to these things. Instead, use them as a springboard to other ideas that are more nearly suited to your particular situation.

- Buy an extra item for the food bank when you shop for groceries this week.
- Box up some clothing for the local shelter, not those things that are already worn out, but clothing in good condition that someone else would be happy to wear.
- Bake some muffins and give them to a busy mom just because.

---

15. Psalm 26:8.
16. Acts 20:35.

- Write an extra check to your church or to a charity of your choice.
- Decide to increase your regular giving.
- Write a letter to the editor about a community issue.
- Write a letter to the government to address a matter of social justice.
- Make that phone call to your older relative that you've been postponing.
- Offer to help out with childcare at church instead of waiting to be asked.
- Do a random act of kindness for a stranger.

Give as a way of connecting with God. Acknowledge that everything belongs to God. Realize that giving means more than money or possessions. Give and be free. Celebrate!

10

Praying the Lord's Prayer

As a father has compassion for his children,
so the LORD *has compassion for those who fear him.*
Psalm 103:13

"Come, Lord Jesus, be our guest, and let this food to us be blest." I learned this table grace as a child and repeated it so often that even now as an adult I sometimes pray these same words when I offer a silent prayer before a meal. The words have a comforting rhythm and come quite naturally to me—so automatically, in fact, that I'm tempted to rattle them off without thinking. But when I slow down and focus, when I'm truly present and paying attention, these simple words can carry me more deeply into prayer.

I reflect on Jesus as a guest at my table, how his presence transforms an ordinary meal into an opportunity for communion with God. I am reminded of "our" table. Even when I'm eating alone, I remain part of a community and a world where some take too much and others do not have enough of God's abundance. The words of blessing remind me never to take food for granted, but to receive even leftovers with thanks as a blessing from God. In this way, my childhood prayer has become as heartfelt and personal as any spontaneous come-as-you-are prayer might be, and continues to teach me how to pray.

I still have a lot to learn about the breadth and depth of prayer. How do I pray at six o'clock in the morning when someone calls in crisis? What do I pray for the person who is struggling, who is in such deep pain yet keeps making the kinds of choices that make everything worse? How do I keep praying for the same person, the same situation, over and over and over without getting tired and giving up, without getting bored? How do I pray continually as described in Scripture?[1] What does it mean for prayer to become personal renewal instead of drudgery, to become a joy instead of a burden?

One day Jesus' disciples came to him and asked, "Lord, teach us to pray." As part of the Jewish religious tradition, Jesus' disciples had already been steeped in prayer from childhood, at home and in the temple. Surely they already knew how to pray, and yet they also knew they needed to learn more. So just as other rabbis at that time taught their disciples to pray, as John the Baptist had taught his disciples,[2] Jesus responded by teaching his disciples this prayer:

Journal Prompt

Reflect on your own experience with the Lord's Prayer. If it is new to you, write down your first impressions. If it's familiar, how is it a regular part of your prayer life? Or if not, why not?

> Our Father in heaven, hallowed be your name.
> Your kingdom come. Your will be done, on earth as it is
>   in heaven.
> Give us this day our daily bread.
> And forgive us our debts, as we also have forgiven
>   our debtors.
> And do not bring us to the time of trial, but rescue us
>   from the evil one.[3]

Learning to pray

In the Anglican church that I attended as a teenager, we prayed the Lord's Prayer as part of our morning worship every Sunday,

1. Philippians 1:3-4; Colossians 1:9; 1 Thessalonians 1:2-3; 5:17.
2. Luke 11:1.
3. Matthew 6:9-13, a slightly longer version than Luke 11:2-4.

using the words "forgive us our trespasses as we forgive those who trespass against us," and adding the closing words of praise found in some manuscripts: "For thine is the kingdom, the power, and the glory, for ever and ever. Amen." As with my childhood table grace, the words and rhythm of the Lord's Prayer have become so much a part of me now that I can easily finish the prayer without thinking; instead, I'm learning to slow down to pray it in earnest, reflecting on each phrase, feeling its weight, savoring the language, and making the prayer my own.

In the Sermon on the Mount, just before Jesus teaches his disciples the Lord's Prayer, he warns them to avoid heaping up "empty phrases" or, as the King James Version puts it, to avoid "vain repetitions."[4] I know from my own experience that it's possible even for the Lord's Prayer to become that—to become nothing more than an empty ritual, repeated over and over without real meaning, without reflection or sincerity.

Once a carefully guarded secret in the early church, reserved only for those who were baptized,[5] today the Lord's Prayer turns up in popular culture and advertising—like the website ad for making money online that used the words "Give us our daily bread." Or the hairstyling company that based their ad campaign around the words "thy will be done." Used in these ways, the Lord's Prayer is robbed of its meaning and power.

But not all repetition is useless. In worship not long ago, we sang a Taizé refrain over and over: "Our Father who art in heaven, Our Father who art in heaven, Our Father who art in heaven." In harmony as a congregation, we seemed to move as one from note to note, embodying the unity and community implied by "our" Father. Then over top, the musicians began to improvise with solo violin, cello, voice. "Our Father who art in heaven, Our Father who art in heaven, Our Father who art in heaven."

---

4. Matthew 6:7.
5. Arthur Paul Boers, *Lord, Teach Us to Pray: A New Look at the Lord's Prayer* (Scottdale: Herald Press, 1992), 23.

Although it's commonly known as the Lord's Prayer, I often think of the prayer that Jesus taught as the Disciples' Prayer, given to his disciples for their prayers, and at the same time expressing what it meant for them to be part of God's kingdom. In the ancient household, the father and patriarch always had the last word. In contrast, the Lord's Prayer is addressed to a higher authority in God, our Father. In ancient Roman culture, Caesar was king. In contrast, the Lord's Prayer looks toward another kingdom, with another King who rules over earth and heaven. The Lord's Prayer was at odds with its surrounding culture, and in the ancient world, that meant it could be dangerous to pray the Lord's Prayer.

Today, the Lord's Prayer is just as radical. In a North American culture that tends to focus on the individual and to privatize religion, the Lord's Prayer insists on our Father and addresses the physical and spiritual needs that we have in common with all people. In our human culture, which is all too familiar with politics and power struggles, with broken relationships and abuse, the Lord's Prayer appeals to a perfect Father and King who is compassionate, faithful, protective, and eternal. In the ancient world and today, the Lord's Prayer was and is countercultural. Do we dare to pray this prayer today in all its meaning and power?

Yes, it was repetition, but it was certainly not an empty ritual as we sang our prayer to God, expressed our longing for God, and were drawn into worship. As our song leader explained, "One of the reasons the repetition in Taizé music for me is so powerful is that it reflects God's grace—there's always another chance to 'get it right'—and, musically, the eventual comfort with the repetition allows you to take risks and 'leaps' on top of the repeated chant."

So it is with praying the Lord's Prayer. If we pray it once or occasionally, we may feel we know it. But as we pray it again and again, turning the phrases over and over until they become the cry of our hearts, we gain a deeper appreciation for God's grace and take the leap of faith. "Forgive us our debts as we forgive our debtors"—God's forgiveness always gives us another chance to "get it right." We gain a deeper appreciation for God's power that allows us to take new risks: "for yours is the kingdom, the power, and the glory."

Repetition can also help to develop us as people of prayer when we find prayer difficult. When I'm feeling unfocused and not sure what or how to pray, I know I can always pray the Lord's Prayer. In times of great need and distress, when we're so angry or so depressed or so upset that we can't pray, times when we really need to pray the most but find ourselves avoiding prayer, we can still pray the Lord's Prayer. At those times when prayer seems to make no sense at all, repeating the Lord's Prayer can be our prayer and carry us into God's presence.

A model prayer

It's not exactly clear that Jesus intended the Lord's Prayer to be repeated word for word each time. To his disciples, he said simply, "Pray then in this way,"[6] which could mean that this prayer was meant to be an example, an outline, a model for prayer. After all, the Lord's Prayer appears in Scripture as part of Jesus' teaching about persistence in prayer, answers to prayer, praying in faith, praying in humility, praying and fasting, praying and hypocrisy, praying and forgiveness.[7] As part of this broader teaching, we might understand the Lord's Prayer as a guide to prayer, a model prayer that shows us how to pray.

The Lord's Prayer begins with "Our" Father in heaven. It's not just "my" Father, but "our" Father. It's not a narrow, me-myself-and-I approach to God, but a broad, corporate address that's carried through the rest of the prayer as it speaks of "our" daily bread, "our" debts, delivering "us" from the evil one. From the first word and throughout, the Lord's Prayer is a way of praying that includes other people before our common "Father." God is not a remote being who set the world in

---

6. Matthew 6:9.
7. Matthew 6:1-18; Luke 11:5-13.

motion and then disappeared. God is a good father who has a close relationship with his children. There is a sense of intimacy, and yet a sense of reverence toward our Father "in heaven."

The Lord's Prayer can serve as a reality check for our own prayer life today. If we pray only for ourselves with no thought of others, then our prayers fall short of Jesus' teaching, because the Lord's Prayer is a prayer that includes other people. If we pray to God only in formal terms with formal language, we miss the intimacy of the Lord's Prayer with God as Father. If we pray to God only in familiar terms as our friend and good buddy, we again miss the fullness of Jesus' teaching, for there is also a sense of God's otherness, of God's holiness.

After "Our Father in heaven," the Lord's Prayer continues with seven requests: Hallowed be your name. Your kingdom come. Your will be done. Give us our daily bread. Forgive us our debts. Do not bring us into trial. Deliver us from the evil one. At first glance, these seven requests might seem quite separate, like individual pearls strung together on the same string but otherwise unrelated. But on closer inspection, they fall quite naturally into two groups. The first three requests focus our attention on God: hallowed be "your" name, may "your" kingdom come, may "your" will be done. The last four requests are more about us as human beings: give "us" daily bread, forgive "us," do not bring "us" into trial, deliver "us" from the evil one.

So we might think of the first part of the prayer as centered on God, with the last part focusing more on human concerns, both on our physical needs in terms of daily bread and on our spiritual needs for forgiveness and deliverance from evil. In the Lord's Prayer, Jesus doesn't separate the concerns of God and the concerns of people. He doesn't separate our physical needs from our spiritual needs. He doesn't separate the global need for God's will on earth from the more personal need for food. All these concerns belong together.

In his treatise *On Prayer*, the sixteenth century John Calvin goes even further by insisting that the Lord's Prayer is so "complete in all its parts" that it contains everything that we are to pray for and "omits nothing."[8] Four hundred years later, Simone Weil makes a similar point: "The Our Father contains all possible petitions; we cannot conceive of any prayer not already contained in it."[9]

Again, there's a reality check here for us. If we pray only for ourselves and never for the glory of God, then according to Jesus' teaching our prayers are incomplete. If we pray only for physical needs and neglect the spiritual ones, or pray only for spiritual needs and neglect the physical ones, then our prayers are missing their other half. If we ignore the concerns of the world, then our prayers are simply too small. But if we pray as Jesus taught us, our prayers engage our whole selves and our whole community and world. Our prayers are enlarged and reshaped, and in turn enlarge and reshape us.

Martin Luther's *A Simple Way to Pray* was originally written as a letter to his barber! In it, he outlines his practice of praying through the Lord's Prayer as well as the Ten Commandments and the Creed. "To this day I suckle at the Lord's Prayer like a child, and as an old man eat and drink from it and never get my fill. It is the very best prayer, even better than the psalter, which is so very dear to me. It is surely evident that a real master composed and taught it."

Sacred pause: pray the Lord's Prayer

In keeping with the Lord's Prayer as authentic prayer and as a model for our prayer life today, consider the following options:

(1) Slow down, become quiet, and pray the Lord's Prayer as your prayer today, either from memory if you already know it well, or from Matthew 6:9-13. Reflect on the meaning of each

8. John Calvin, *Institutes of the Christian Religion*, Henry Beveridge, tr., Book III, Chapter XX, "Of Prayer," (1845), 48–49.
9. Simone Weil, *Waiting for God*, Emma Craufurd, tr. (New York: Harper & Row, 1951), 226.

phrase. How do you experience God as "our Father in heaven"? Do you long for God more intimately, or do you need a greater sense of reverence for God's otherness? For each of the seven petitions of the Lord's Prayer, allow God to bring specific situations or people to mind and offer them back to God in prayer. End with the doxology: "For yours is the kingdom, the power, and the glory for ever. Amen."

(2) Reflect on your own prayer life in light of the Lord's Prayer. How do you normally address God, or does this vary for you? What does your form of address tell you about the intimacy or reverence you experience in your relationship with God? Do you include both God's glory and human concerns in your prayers? Both physical and spiritual concerns? Both personal and global? What would you need to add to your prayers to become more like the Lord's Prayer?

(3) Write a prayer in your journal that mirrors the Lord's Prayer, beginning with an address that expresses both God's nearness and God's otherness. Think of three requests that focus on God. Then add one statement addressing a physical need, and three statements about spiritual well-being. End with an expression of praise.

Mirroring the Lord's Prayer

The Lord's Prayer says a lot in remarkably few words, conveying both intimacy and reverence for God, embracing physical, spiritual, personal, and global concerns. Here is one attempt at mirroring the Lord's Prayer:

O God, Creator of the Universe and my Closest Friend,
Reveal yourself in this broken world,
Pour out your compassion,
and reign over us.
Feed those who are hungry,
Free those who are oppressed,
Forgive us our failures,
And find us again and again.
All praise to you—
today and to eternity—Amen.

11

Making Music

<hr />

I will solve my riddle to the music of the harp.
Psalm 49:4

"If a tree falls in a forest with no one there to hear it, will it still make a sound?" I heard this classic question for the first time when I was a teenager, and my immediate and naive answer was, "Of course. Even if there was no human being to hear the sound, there would be deer, or a bird or a bug, and besides, God would be in the forest."

I now realize that the question is more of a philosophical one about the nature of perception and reality. In terms of human science, the answer is no. The tree falling in the forest makes the molecules in the air vibrate, but it's only when the vibration reaches the ear that our brain creates the sound. In the same way, it's the brain that creates music, translating the vibrations in our ears into melody and rhythm.

That makes all of us music-makers, even if we don't play an instrument or can't carry a tune. The design of the human brain and the science of sound waves make me marvel at the wonder of God's creation.[1]

The power of music

In 1697, English playwright and poet William Congreve wrote *The Mourning Bride*, which begins with Almeria, Princess of Granada, speaking to her attendant:

<hr />

1. Daniel J. Levitin, *This Is Your Brain on Music: The Science of a Human Obsession* (New York: Dutton, 2006), 22.

> Musick has Charms to sooth a savage Breast,
> To soften Rocks, or bend a knotted Oak.

The first line is often quoted, and just as frequently misquoted, to soothe a savage "beast," but either way the point is most often to highlight the power of music to soothe troubled emotions, to smooth out the rough places in our minds and hearts, to calm restless thoughts, to ease depression, and relieve anxiety.

But while Almeria's first line above is often used to point out the benefits of music, what many don't realize is that it's actually part of a longer speech about how music was unable to provide her with comfort. Just a few lines later, Almeria says,

> What then am I? Am I more senseless grown
> Than Trees, or Flint? O force of constant Woe!
> 'Tis not in Harmony to calm my Griefs.[2]

In other words, music was not able to soothe her. For all its "charms," music also has its limits.

In many places today, music seems to function more as background filler than anything else. In the mall, in stores, in elevators, at the dentist's office, in restaurants, there always seems to be music. Perhaps it's meant to be calming in some situations or to encourage sales in others, but I wonder if anyone is really paying attention. At least I know that it's rare for me to notice anything more than the wash of sound in the background.

But music as spiritual practice is much more than music as background noise. Instead, it's another way that we can be attentive to God in daily life, to pray, to offer our thanks and praise, to be renewed.

One church worker makes a point of listening to Taizé-style music while driving between pastoral visits and other appointments: "Sometimes I simply listen; other times I sing along.

---

2. William Congreve, *The Mourning Bride*, Act I, Scene I, 1697.

It's a way of calming my spirit and helping me to rest in God."
A refugee support worker uses music as an outlet for the pain
from hearing the stories of refugees and displaced people. "On
my drive home, I always listen to loud music," she said. "You
see, I have to, as a way of dealing with the stress."

In Scripture, King Saul turned to music when he was feeling tormented and unwell. That's how he first met David, who
was a shepherd, a warrior, and also
a skilled musician on the harp.
Whenever Saul fell into torment,
David would be brought to court
to play for him, and Saul would
find relief. But even David's fine
musicianship had its limits. One
day while David was playing his
harp, Saul found no relief and

Journal Prompt

**What role does music play in your
life? Do you have a favorite type of
music? Does your preference for
different style(s) of music change
depending on your mood or
circumstances?**

became so agitated that he tried to pin David to the wall with a
spear. Fortunately David was able to escape, and Saul ended up
driving his spear into the wall instead.[3]

Music is a regular part of worship throughout Scripture: "O
come, let us sing to the LORD."[4] "Sing to the LORD a new song."[5]
On the night of his arrest, Jesus and his disciples sing a hymn
before going out to the Mount of Olives.[6] The early church is told,
"Let the word of Christ dwell in you richly; teach and admonish
one another in all wisdom; and with gratitude in your hearts sing
psalms, hymns, and spiritual songs to God."[7] In Revelation, there
is a new song,[8] the song of Moses,[9] and the song of the Lamb.[10]

3. 1 Samuel 16:14-23; 19:9-10.
4. Psalm 95:1; cf. Psalm 13:6; 147:7.
5. Psalm 149:1; cf. Psalm 96:1; 98:1.
6. Mark 14:26.
7. Colossians 3:16; cf. Ephesians 5:18-20; James 5:13.
8. Revelation 5:9; cf. 14:3
9. Revelation 15:3.
10. Revelation 15:3.

In fact, music is such a powerful part of worship that it's sometimes equated with worship even to the exclusion of Scripture, prayer, and sermon. "We'll begin with worship and then move on to the sermon," said one young song leader. But the singing that begins our worship is only one element, along with sermon, Scripture, prayer, silence, drama, children's story, and many other expressions directed toward God. Worship includes all of these elements and more. And the worship team is not only those who plan and lead the singing, but everyone involved in planning and leading the entire worship time. Music is an important part of worship, but it's not the whole thing.

> **Be filled with the Spirit,
> as you sing psalms and hymns and
>   spiritual songs among yourselves,
> singing and making melody to the
>   Lord in your hearts,
> giving thanks to God the Father at
>   all times
> and for everything in the name of
>   our Lord Jesus Christ
>   (Ephesians 5:18b-20).**

Music as spiritual practice is also just one element and not the whole thing. The power of music to move us and affect us deeply means that we can also be moved in ways that may be unhealthy, that may be spiritually harmful. In popular music, lyrics that promote racial hatred, that denigrate women, that advocate violence, that glorify war and murder are especially troubling. The tune may be catchy, the beat may be thrilling, the gangsta image may be compelling, but the power of music can be used for evil instead of good. For healthy spirituality, music is not everything, but it needs to be weighed also by the Spirit of God, through Scripture, prayer, and good discernment.

Most often in Scripture, music is part of celebration. When the Hebrew people successfully pass through the sea on dry land, Miriam and the women celebrate with tambourines and singing."[11] After David becomes king and brings the ark of God

---

11. Exodus 15:20-21.

back from the land of the Philistines, there is a great celebration "with songs and lyres and harps and tambourines and castanets and cymbals."[12] In Jesus' story of the prodigal son, the young man's return is celebrated with music and dancing.[13]

In contrast, as Job suffers the loss of family, possessions, and even his own health, he says, "My lyre is turned to mourning, and my pipe to the voice of those who weep."[14] As the prophet Ezekiel pronounces judgment on the city of Tyre, as he foretells the destruction of the city, he says that God "will silence the music of your songs; the sound of your lyres shall be heard no more."[15]

"I can't imagine a home without an instrument," my piano tuner once said to me. I suppose that no home is ever really without, as long as there is a voice that can be raised in song, as long as there is a box or a tabletop or any other object that can be turned into a drumming surface. I once saw a group of performers make music from an assortment of garbage cans, brooms, and old hubcaps. There is music all around us. So for Ezekiel to warn of the absence of music was a measure of the depth of the coming desolation. It would truly be the day the music died.

> **Make a joyful noise to the LORD, all the earth;**
> **break forth into joyous song and sing praises.**
> **Sing praises to the LORD with the lyre,**
> **with the lyre and the sound of melody.**
> **With trumpets and the sound of the horn**
> **make a joyful noise before the King, the LORD (Psalm 98:4-6).**

Music as personal prayer

When I was in high school, I taught myself to play the guitar, and for the next several years I would spend hours writing my own songs as a personal form of prayer:

---

12. 2 Samuel 6:5.
13. Luke 15:25.
14. Job 30:31.
15. Ezekiel 26:13.

Darkness falls, the city sleeps,
yet awake my vigil keep.
Silence stills me, peace fulfills me,
in this quiet moment.
I bring no offering, no holy sacrifice,
No good deeds, no fine-turned phrase,
No golden notes to sing your praise.

Just a broken heart and a spirit fully spent,
Seeking shelter in your wings where I will be content.

—AY

My songs never did make it out of the privacy of my room,
but that didn't matter then or now. As I look back, I realize that
they were another form of sacred pause—away from my family
and friends to spend time alone with God, away from school
work, away from any of the other do's and don'ts that were a
part of my life:

Through my window, deep the night—
here, within, there shines a light.
Earth, still sleep on, I will keep on
savoring this moment.
I ask no miracle, no intercession make,
No plea for help, no thing to bless, no questioning to
    lay to rest,
Just let me be stayed on you and sit here quietly,
For the refuge of my God seems miracle to me.

—AY

It's been a long time since I've written a song, but I find
that music still plays an important part in my spiritual life. In
worshiping with others, I relate to both traditional hymns and
contemporary Christian songs. When I'm on my own, I resonate with many different styles of music. Vivaldi's *Four Seasons*
has been a long-time favorite. Even though the set of four
concertos is not overtly religious (there is no mention of God

in the accompanying sonnets), I find that the music always lifts my spirit and draws my thoughts to God, who is, after all, the Creator of the seasons. Other favorites include Gregorian chant, Van Morrison's *Hymns to the Silence*, anything by U2, and many other pieces, both sacred and what some might consider secular, that have the power to refresh, renew, and turn my thoughts to God.

These days my favorite musical pause is playing the piano. Like my guitar songs that never made it out of the house, my piano playing is also a form of personal prayer, definitely not for public consumption. The way I play is more of a "joyful noise"[16] than anything else. I don't play anything with too many sharps or flats or sixteenth notes. I don't worry about wrong notes or awkward fingering and freely skip over sections that seem too hard. At times my noise is not even joyful, but deliberately heavy-handed, discordant, and harsh according to my mood. I find it good therapy to play piano badly, to take time out from all the things I try to do well, and simply play it as it comes. That too is part of my prayer and spiritual life.

Sleep as spiritual practice

In his book on *The Attentive Life*, Leighton Ford notes how difficult it is to be spiritually attentive when we are over-tired. "Is sleep a spiritual exercise?" he asks. "Yes," he writes, "because we are not just spiritual beings. We are embodied spirits." Since we are both physical and spiritual beings, we need both physical and spiritual rest. Sleep provides both—"for our bodies and for the renewal of our souls." Leighton Ford, *The Attentive Life* (Downer's Grove: IVP Books, 2008), 60.

There are limits, of course. I don't always feel better after I play the piano or listen to good music. The riddles of my life are not always solved so neatly. But like the refugee support worker, in music I sometimes find respite from the stress of life. Sometimes I find clarity on what I need to do and the energy to

---

16. Psalm 100:1.

go and do it. In the meantime, as with all spiritual disciplines, I wait for God. "I will sing and make melody to the LORD. Hear, O LORD, when I cry aloud, be gracious to me and answer me!"[17]

Sacred pause: rejoice in the sound of music

(1) *Listening.* If you normally have music playing in the background without really listening to it, try bringing music into the foreground as your spiritual practice. Choose a piece of music that lifts your spirit and helps you focus on God. Sit or lie down in a comfortable position, and close your eyes. Breathe slowly and deeply, and take time to listen. If you find yourself dozing off, give yourself permission to rest. Sleep can be a spiritual practice too.

If you're on the road a lot, you might want to follow the practice of the church worker who listened to music between appointments. Instead of listening to the traffic news, listen to music that calms your soul. Instead of jumping out of the car immediately when you arrive, take that extra moment to allow the song to finish, collect your thoughts, and then carry on with your day.

(2) *Walking/dancing.* If you prefer to be more physically active, use your CD or MP3 player to combine your listening with a walk (chapter 6). Or try some creative movement or dance moves. Do they assist you in an attitude of prayer and worship, or are they a distraction?

(3) *Making music.* If you play an instrument regularly, making music may feel more like work than a sacred pause. But try playing a piece just for fun. Or play at a different time of day than usual. Try selecting a new melody. Set aside your usual expectations.

---

17. Psalm 27:6b-7.

12

Fasting

For he satisfies the thirsty,
and the hungry he fills with good things.
Psalm 107:9

It's almost automatic for me to turn on the radio whenever I drive anywhere by myself. I get into the car, put on my seatbelt, turn the ignition, turn on the radio—almost all in one motion. I listen to just about anything from the news to the traffic report, talk shows, rock music, classical or international music, country, even my husband's favorite sports station if that's what happens to be on. For a short drive around town, I may not bother to change the station, but on longer drives or whenever I get stuck in traffic, I find myself restlessly switching from station to station to keep myself entertained.

Instead of a food fast one year, I decided to give up listening to the car radio for Lent. In church tradition, the six weeks of Lent that lead up to Easter Sunday are often associated with repentance and reflection on the suffering and death of Jesus. Giving up something for Lent, like coffee or chocolate or listening to the car radio, is meant to serve as a reminder that Jesus gave up his life on the cross. Compared to his sacrifice, whatever we might give up is small, and yet this form of fasting can also be powerful. It's amazing to me how giving up something that's actually quite trivial can help give clarity to what's really important in life. Like slowing down and becoming quiet, fasting is another way of creating space in my life that helps me listen to God in a new way.

So I decided to fast by giving up my car radio for those six weeks. No more automatically pressing the power button every time I got into the car. No more restlessly switching from one station to another whenever I got bored. No cheating with CDs or MP3 or any other kind of music or recordings while I was on the road. No breaking my fast for six whole weeks, including Sundays.

For the first few days, I found myself automatically turning on the radio anyway, then remembering my resolve, and turning it off again. But then I gradually got used to my new routine: geting into the car, putting on my seatbelt, turning the ignition, and going. I gradually got used to the silence as I drove. I began to enjoy being more focused on the road and on my surroundings. I began to think more, to pray more, and I no longer automatically reached for the radio. In fact, not listening to the radio quickly became easy.

But about the end of week four, I found myself missing my car radio. I wondered what the armchair analysts were saying on my favorite political commentary show. Driving home alone at night, I missed the company of familiar voices and the comfort of good music. When I got stuck in traffic, I was tempted to listen to the traffic report "just this once."

But I didn't. After all, that was the point of fasting. It was at those times that I learned more about how giving up something can help make room for something more. Not listening to my radio was a small sacrifice, but it did remind me of Jesus' far greater sacrifice of his life on the cross. It made me realize that Jesus can be the best company whenever I am lonely, that I can turn to God not just when I'm stuck in traffic, but whenever I feel stuck in my life. If I had done my usual thing and filled that time with the sound of my radio, I might have missed that deepening sense of God's presence.

Why fast?

When I had surgery a number of years ago, I experienced a different kind of fasting: no food or drink, not even water, in preparation for general anaesthesia. Some kinds of blood tests also require fasting, and some people may fast to lose or maintain their weight. In some religious traditions, fasting may mean not eating until the sun goes down, or not eating meat on Fridays.

In Scripture, fasting is often a sign of mourning. After the men buried the bodies of Saul and his sons, they fasted for seven days.[1] Nehemiah broke down weeping, fasting, and praying as he mourned over the people of Jerusalem and the destruction of the city.[2] Fasting as a sign of mourning included fasting as a sign of repentance and mourning over sin. So when the people of Israel put away their false idols and turned back to God, they held a day of fasting.[3] When the people of Nineveh believed God, they also fasted in repentance and prayed earnestly for God to spare them.[4]

Fasting coupled with prayer was part of David's own personal experience as he fasted and prayed desperately for God to spare the life of his son.[5] Mordecai, Esther and her maids, and all the Jews in Susa were fasting and praying as Esther prepared to petition the king to change his edict against the Jews.[6] Fasting and prayer were part of the corporate experience of Ezra and his people as they prayed for safe journey on their way to Jerusalem.[7]

Besides these times of fasting and prayer prompted by personal or national crisis, regular fasting was also seen as a form of piety and faithfulness to God. The prophet Anna spent her time in worship at the temple, "with fasting and prayer night

---

1. 1 Samuel 31:11-13.
2. Nehemiah 1:4.
3. 1 Samuel 7:6.
4. Jonah 3:5ff.
5. 2 Samuel 12:16.
6. Esther 4.
7. Ezra 8:21-23.

and day."[8] Jesus began his ministry with a time of fasting in the wilderness.[9] He seemed to assume that his disciples would practice fasting when he gave them instructions in the Sermon on the Mount: "when you fast, put oil on your head and wash your face."[10] The early church practiced fasting and praying together as part of discerning and calling mission workers and leaders.[11]

And yet for all these positive examples of fasting as expressions of faith, there were also those who spoke against this spiritual discipline. The prophet Isaiah writes:

> Look, you fast only to quarrel and to fight and to strike with a wicked fist. Such fasting as you do today will not make your voice heard on high. Is such the fast that I choose, a day to humble oneself? Is it to bow down the head like a bulrush, and to lie in sackcloth and ashes? Will you call this a fast, a day acceptable to the Lord? Is not this the fast that I choose: to loose the bonds of injustice, to undo the thongs of the yoke, to let the oppressed go free, and to break every yoke? Is it not to share your bread with the hungry, and bring the homeless poor into your house; when you see the naked, to cover them, and not to hide yourself from your own kin?[12]

For Isaiah, fasting is not simply abstaining from food or drink. A true fast means practicing justice and compassion, sharing what you have with others. Zechariah adds that we are to show kindness and mercy to others, to treat those on the margins of society with justice.[13]

So if I fast and become grumpy and rude to others because of my low blood sugar, that's not a true fast. I may as well have

---

8. Luke 2:37.
9. Matthew 4:2.
10. Matthew 6:17.
11. Acts 13:2-3; 14:23.
12. Isaiah 58:4-7.
13. Zechariah 7:4-11.

something to eat or drink and act with kindness and mercy. If I fast, but ignore those who are hungry and homeless and fail to take care of my own family, then fasting is only a ritual, and not the kind of fast recognized by God. Fasting is not only about *not* eating or *not doing* certain things; fasting is also about what we *do*. It's not only about how we treat ourselves and our own bodies; fasting is also about how we treat other people, especially those who are most in need.

Jesus adds another element of caution as he addresses those who make a public show of their fast-ing. He tells the story of one man

> And whenever you fast, do not look dismal, like the hypocrites, for they disfigure their faces so as to show others that they are fasting. Truly I tell you, they have received their reward. But when you fast, put oil on your head and wash your face, so that your fasting may be seen not by others but by your Father who is in secret; and your Father who sees in secret will reward you (Matthew 6:16-18).

who prayed with pride, "I fast twice a week; I give a tenth of all my income," and compares him unfavorably to a second man who simply prayed for God's mercy.[14] In the Sermon on the Mount he tells his disciples that fasting was not meant for show. Although fasting was physical, it was also an inward spiritual discipline. The reward for fasting was not the admiration of others, but a more intimate relationship with God.

Like any other spiritual discipline, fasting can become a point of pride. If I need to tell people what I'm giving up for Lent, then I'm quite likely doing it for the wrong reasons. If I need everyone to know that I've started fasting one day a week, I might just as well skip the fasting and pray for God's mercy. Yes, there's a place for accountability and sharing with others for mutual support. Yes, there's a place for personal testimony. But there's also a difference between good accountability and showing off, between sharing our experience with others and needing to pat ourselves on the back.

---

14. Luke 18:9-14.

The real challenge of fasting is not so much what we're going to give up. The real question is, when we are no longer reaching for the coffee pot, what will we reach for? When our fingers are no longer curled around the TV remote, what will we grasp instead? Will we practice justice, kindness, and mercy? Will we become proud of our fasting whether it's from food or technology or something else? How will we deal with the inevitable temptations? Can we go forward with the confidence that God will fill us with good things?

Fasting as self-denial

Of all the spiritual disciplines, I often think that fasting is one of the easiest to weave into daily life. After all, I can not eat whether I'm at home or away, whether I'm running errands or working. I can squeeze in not eating any time. It's faster to fast than to sit down and eat a healthy meal. But skipping lunch because I'm too busy to eat is not the same as fasting. It's not about repentance or mourning. It doesn't have anything to do with prayer or seeking God's guidance. It's not related to justice or kindness. So simply skipping a meal is not the same as fasting as spiritual practice.

What are you giving up for Lent? "Eating liver," says one person. "A trip around the world," says another. It's easy to abstain from foods that we don't eat anyway, or to give up things that we're not going to do anyway. But that misses the point, for fasting as spiritual practice means a

---

Too much of a good thing

In fasting, some people may choose to target a bad habit, so they might fast from gossip, or decide to give up their daily doughnut. But just as often, fasting may mean giving up something not because it's harmful or unhealthy, but because it's just too much of a good thing. Our bodies need good food, but too much good food is actually unhealthy. Technology can be used to build community, but relying too much on technology may actually hamper our personal relationships. In the face of excess, fasting reminds us of the need for moderation, for good choices, and for good boundaries.

deliberate self-denial—not so much to give up some *thing*, as to give up our *selves*.

When I give up my car radio, it's not so much about the radio as it is about my desire. When I give up chocolate, it's not so much about that delicious dark chocolate studded with almonds as it is about my desire. So if I give up liver that I don't like anyway, there's no self-denial involved, and no fasting.

A true fast also includes justice, mercy, and kindness, because they involve self-denial. Instead of keeping everything for myself, I practice self-denial by sharing with others. Instead of tailgating the car in front of me and honking my horn because the driver is moving too slowly, I can practice self-denial and be kind to the stranger. These things are not the same as giving up television for a week, but they are another way of saying no to self.

Practiced this way, fasting as self-denial can open us to a deeper awareness of God's presence, make room for prayer, and even improve the way we relate to other people. Instead of constantly filling ourselves so that we become overloaded physically and spiritually, we can let go of our over-full plates and our over-full schedules and be free. As we say no to ourselves, we say yes to God and receive all that God has in store for us.

Sacred pause: plan your fast

Fasting requires preparation, so take time to plan. Consider your own situation and what it might mean to deny yourself. What would you miss? And for how long? It might be a partial fast where you keep eating normally, everything except the junk food. Or it might be a full food fast for a whole day where you don't eat anything but keep well hydrated with water. For Lent one year, my husband gave up following the sports news. A group of church youth did a 48-hour media fast where they unplugged from all electronic media. Other fasts might mean abstaining from your favorite social network, or texting, or shopping. Whatever you choose, fasting as spiritual practice involves some kind of self-denial.

At the same time, like all spiritual disciplines, fasting takes practice. So don't go for a full food fast if you've never fasted before. Start with giving up just one type of food or one meal. For some, even that might be too physically demanding, so be aware of your own health and physical limits, and restrict yourself to a nonfood fast as needed. Fasting from yelling at your kids, fasting from gossip, fasting from movies, and other kinds of nonfood fasts can be just as effective.

Journal Prompt

Think of a time of fasting or self-denial in your life. What prompted you at that time? How did you feel? What did you learn?

As you consider the type of fast you will practice, consider also the length of time. Some might find a 48-hour media fast long enough; others might need more time. Some might find giving up chocolate for a week too short and for six weeks of Lent just about right. Unlike the man in Jesus' story who was proud of fasting twice a week, fasting one day a week may be quite enough. I found that giving up my car radio for the first four weeks of Lent came quite easily to me, and the challenge and growth came mainly in the last two weeks.

As you plan for your fast, consider combining spiritual disciplines. If you normally buy lunch every Friday and decide to fast from that expense, consider coupling that with an equivalent offering to the local food bank or other community organization. If you decide on an email-free day, use the extra time to pray or immerse yourself in Scripture. Consider how your fast will include acts of justice and mercy. Perhaps you could take your donation to the food bank, or send a card to someone who is ill.

When the time comes for your fast, don't focus so much on the fasting that you forget the meaning of self-denial and reflecting on the sacrifice of Jesus. Instead of concentrating on the thing you're giving up, turn your attention to God's presence and promise to fill you with good things. If you break your fast inadvertently—as I often did in the first few days of my car radio fast, don't give up and don't berate yourself. Simply return to your fast and carry on.

13

Having Fun

How precious is your steadfast love, O God!
All people may take refuge in the shadow of your wings.
They feast on the abundance of your house,
and you give them drink from the river of your delights.
For with you is the fountain of life; in your light we see light.
Psalm 36:7-9

A life of faith is not all fasting and discipline. The self-control that is part of the self-denial of fasting is just one part of the fruit of the Spirit: "love, joy, peace, patience, kindness, generosity, faithfulness, gentleness, and self-control."[1] With love and joy in first and second place, there is plenty of room in this list for feasting and enjoying life! Even John Calvin, for all his sixteenth-century stern reputation, admits that it was never "forbidden to laugh, or to be full, or to add new to old and hereditary possessions, or to be delighted with music, or to drink wine."[2]

Jesus himself was sometimes accused of going to too many parties. He performed his first public miracle at a wedding celebration.[3] He was frequently hosted at dinner parties.[4] He had a good sense of humor with stories about trying to take a speck out of someone's eye while having a log in your own eye,[5] and a

---

1. Galatians 5:22-23.
2. John Calvin, *Institutes of the Christian Religion* III, 19:9.
3. John 2:1-10.
4. Luke 19:5-10; John 12:2ff.
5. Matthew 7:3-5.

camel going through the eye of a needle.[6] Behind his back, his critics complained that he ate and drank too much.[7]

Jesus was well aware of what people were saying. On the one hand, they criticized John the Baptist for his ascetic way of life, and on the other, they criticized Jesus for indulging too much. They were not satisfied either way. Others were frankly curious.

> But to what will I compare this generation? It is like children sitting in the marketplaces and calling to one another, "We played the flute for you, and you did not dance; we wailed, and you did not mourn." For John came neither eating nor drinking, and they say, "He has a demon"; the Son of Man came eating and drinking, and they say, "Look, a glutton and a drunkard, a friend of tax collectors and sinners!" Yet wisdom is vindicated by her deeds (Matthew 11:16-19).

"Why do we and the Pharisees fast often, but your disciples do not fast?" asked John's disciples. Jesus replied by comparing himself to a bridegroom with his disciples as his wedding guests. Their shared life was a time of joy, so fasting as a sign of mourning would wait until after his death. In the meantime, they were celebrating![8]

Jesus was not at all antilife or antijoy. His birth was announced as joy to the world.[9] He described salvation as entering into the joy of the Lord.[10] He loved children[11] and spent time with friends.[12] His mission was to bring abundant life[13] and complete joy.[14] In the early church, the followers of Jesus continued in a spirit of joy; there was joy in believing and being part of God's kingdom, [15] joy at being healed,[16] the joy of Christian community.[17]

6. Mark 10:25.
7. Luke 7:34; cf. Matthew 11:19.
8. Matthew 9:14-15.
9. Luke 2:10-11.
10. Matthew 25:21, 23.
11. Mark 10:13-16.
12. Luke 10:38-42; John 11.
13. John 10:10.
14. John 15:11; 16:24; 17:13.
15. Acts 15:3; Romans 14:17; 15:13.
16. Acts 8:8.
17. Philippians 1:4; 2:2; 1 Thessalonians 2:19-20.

With all this joy in Scripture, I'm not sure why the reputation of the Christian church tends to be just the opposite, so serious and even joyless in the eyes of some. As Jesuit priest and author James Martin notes, "Joy, humor and laughter are underappreciated values in the spiritual life," and yet he argues that joy is "an essential element in one's own relationship with God."[18] Certainly in Scripture, the presence of joy is a sign of the presence of God.

Journal Prompt

How would you respond to the young woman who thought rioting was fun? How do you discern between good fun and bad fun?

Of course, joy is not quite the same thing as having fun—and having fun can be defined in different ways. One year, when the Vancouver Canucks lost the final hockey game for the Stanley Cup, rioting broke out in downtown Vancouver with vehicles being overturned and set on fire. In the aftermath of the riot, I heard an interview on the radio with a young woman who had been involved. "Why were you there?" she was asked. "Oh I wanted to be there, just to go with the flow," she said. "I thought it would be fun."

A public riot is definitely a different kind of fun, not related to the fun of a major sports event, and not at all related to the joy of Jesus. There is a big difference between the kind of destructive fun that's not really fun at all and the kind of fun that is creative, life-giving, and honoring to God.

Smiling at God

For spring break one year, my husband and I traveled south to Phoenix, Arizona, and the surrounding area. I loved the desert air, the cactus, the open spaces, and most of all I loved our visit to the Chapel of the Holy Cross set high up in the red rock of Sedona. We parked down below for a great view of the huge

---

18. James Martin, Baccalaureate Address, University of Pennsylvania, May 15, 2011, http://www.upenn.edu/almanac/volumes/v57/n34/bacc-martin.html.

cross rising above the rock, then walked up the steep path to the entrance on the other side. The chapel was built as a place of worship and a work of art, as "a spiritual fortress so charged with God" [19] that it spurs us Godward. I felt that as I entered the chapel to pray. It was a deeply moving time in a beautiful setting in the middle of a wonderful vacation. As we lingered outside the chapel for a little while longer, I noticed a patch of pansies in the garden with a small sign: "Please don't pick us—we're smiling at God."

I felt as if I was smiling at God that day, and I am sure that God was smiling on me. At least, that's how I understand the traditional blessing: "The LORD bless you and keep you; the LORD make his face to shine upon you, and be gracious to you; the LORD lift up his countenance upon you, and give you peace." [20] The God who loves us is not a joyless, rigid figure, but One who looks on us with blessing, who rejoices when we turn Godward, [21] who shines—or shall I say, smiles—on us. The joy of the Lord is our strength. [22]

St. Therese of Liseux was a Carmelite nun in the nineteenth century who began one of her poems with "A flower is the smile of God." [23] I can just imagine God's delight in creation, creating tiny white snowdrops and showy purple passion flowers, a profusion of wild orchids and a field of bright red poppies—an endless variety of beautiful flowers including the pansies at the Chapel of the Holy Cross—all created for the sheer enjoyment of their creation. So too with the rest of plant and animal life, the diversity of human beings, the creation of stars and planets that we can only imagine. God the Creator looked over all

---

19. Posted at the Chapel of the Holy Cross.
20. Numbers 6:24-26.
21. Luke 15:3-10.
22. Nehemiah 8:10.
23. Felicity Leng, comp., *Invincible Spirits: A Thousand Years of Women's Spiritual Writings* (Grand Rapids: Eerdmans, 2006), 44.

creation and pronounced it "very good."[24] How appropriate then for us to smile back at God and to enjoy God's very good creation.

Play time, party time!

One way of enjoying God's creation is through play. As Gordon Houser writes in *Present Tense*,

> Play is without goals, other than to engage in play. Children don't say, Hey, it would improve our health if we played tag. Neither do they say, Let's play chess because it may improve my mental powers and help me get into a good college. . . .
>
> How then should we play? We can enter activities we enjoy—whether basketball, sewing, doing crosswords or cooking—with a sense of enjoying that activity for itself. This is called autotelic behavior [i.e., done for its own sake]. You can also call it having fun.[25]

A friend of mine shares my love of the *New York Times* crossword puzzle, but she doesn't understand why I also like number games such as *Sudoku* and *Ken Ken*. "I don't understand those," she says. "What's the point?" And that's the thing. There really isn't any point, except to do them for their own sake, just for fun, for the sheer joy of numbers, just as I like crossword puzzles for the sheer joy of words. For me, these are pure play. I'm not scrambling to meet a deadline; I don't worry if I make mistakes and have to cross things out; it's okay even if I can't quite finish. I have fun anyway.

In Scripture, celebrating is another way of having fun. Jesus tells the story of a young man who presumes to ask for his share of the inheritance while his father is still alive. He leaves home,

---

24. Genesis 1:31.
25. Gordon Houser, *Present Tense: A Mennonite Spirituality* (Telford, PA: Cascadia Publishing House, 2011), 95–96.

spends all that he has, and becomes so desperate that he returns home, repentant and hopeful that his father might receive him back as a hired hand. On the son's return, his father is so overjoyed that he puts on a great celebration: the best clothes for his son, with a ring on his finger and sandals on his feet; servants to prepare a fine feast; music and dancing. Everyone is having a lot of fun!

Everyone, that is, except for the son's older brother. When his younger brother returns home, the older brother is out working in the fields. By the time he finishes his work and returns home, the party is already in full swing. What's going on? he asks. His younger brother has returned home? The party is for the prodigal who has wasted his share of the inheritance? The older brother becomes so angry that he refuses to enter the house. He refuses to join the celebration even when his father comes out to plead with him. [26]

Is it fun, or is it hard work?

One woman loves gardening and happily spends hours digging in the dirt. Another sees gardening as a chore and would rather do just about anything else. One man enjoys mountain climbing, another spends long hours doing woodwork in his basement. One person's fun may well be another person's hard work or pet peeve. What's fun for you?

I have a lot of sympathy for the older brother. While the younger brother was out wasting money, the older brother was at home and hard at work. As a good son, he had always followed his father's direction, yet his father had never put on a party for him and his friends. How then could he celebrate with his younger brother? It just wasn't fair. Jesus leaves the story unfinished, with the celebration going on inside and the father and older brother still talking outside.

From the outset, it seems that the younger brother wanted to have fun with his inheritance, actually thought he was having fun until everything was gone, including his money and his

---

26. Luke 15:11-32.

fun friends. But his real fun only came at the end, once he had learned his lesson, returned to his father, and they could celebrate together. In contrast, the older brother was working hard and acting responsibly, but all the while feeling jealous of his younger brother's freedom and growing more and more resentful. He wasn't having any fun but, as he later discovers, he had been denying himself unnecessarily; everything that belonged to his father was his. He could have had a party any time.

As I let my imagination wander, I like to finish the story with the older brother deciding to join the party after all. He listens to his father and comes to a new understanding of the meaning of family. He is able to set aside his anger against his father and his younger brother and reconciles with them both. He changes from his work clothes into a fresh robe, and he has a great time at the party—eating, dancing, and laughing with genuine joy at the return of his younger brother. And the next night, the father puts on another celebration for the older brother and all his friends.

What is your attitude toward play and party time? Do you identify more with the younger brother whose first impulse is to indulge himself and later repent? Or are you more like the older brother whose work ethic, sense of responsibility, jealousy, and anger prevent him from having fun?

For all their differences, the two brothers actually have a lot in common. Both are at a distance when the father comes to meet them: the younger son making his way back from a distant country, the older son making his way back from working in the fields. Both are part of the same family and deeply loved: the father running to meet the younger son then going out to plead with his older son. In the same way, God loves us—whatever our past has been, whatever our present. God reaches out to us when we are far off. Come, join God's party!

Sacred pause: enjoy yourself

Two friends recall hearing theology professor Tim Perry talk about ancient Lenten practices that included both "mortification" (i.e., practices of self-denial like fasting) and "vivification" (i.e., practices that are life-giving), so that year, instead of simply giving up something for Lent, they decided also to add something that would be life-giving. That's when they started reading one poem a day for each day of Lent: *Love Poems from God*, which includes the poetry of St. Francis of Assisi and St. Teresa of Avila, poetry by Jean Janzen, David Wright, and many others.

In *The Sound of Music*, Maria sings a list of some of her favorite things: "raindrops on roses, whiskers on kittens," all the way down to "silver white winters that melt into springs." My own list is far less poetic: hot chocolate on a cold winter's day, a starry night sky, cherry blossoms, ladybugs, the smell of the ocean, leaves crunching underfoot, fresh towels, candlelight, reading in bed, children laughing, church bells. What are some of your favorite things? Poetry? Raindrops on roses? Something else? What do you find refreshing, life-giving, and fun?

As you reflect on these things, give thanks to God as the giver of every good gift.[27] Acknowledge God as the source of each joy and blessing. Then take some time to experience one of your favorite things. Do something you enjoy but don't get to do every day. It might be only for a few moments, but receive that time and experience as a gift from God.

If you feel guilty about enjoying yourself, remember that God delights in you! As the psalmist says, "He brought me out into a broad place; he delivered me, because he delighted in me."[28] In turn, you may also "Take delight in the Lord, and he will give you the desires of your heart."[29] "This is the day that the Lord has made; let us rejoice and be glad in it."[30]

---

27. James 1:17.
28. Psalm 18:19; cf. Psalm 22:8; 35:27; Isaiah 62:4; 65:19.
29. Psalm 37:4.
30. Psalm 118:24.

14

Paying Attention

———————

May my meditation be pleasing to him,
for I rejoice in the LORD.
Psalm 104:34

When we first moved into our town house, I was aware
that our two-car garage was quite a bit narrower than
the garage I was used to at our former house. So each time I
parked my little Saturn, I was mindful to leave enough room
for my husband's slightly larger Prius, and each time I backed
out, I was careful not to get too close to his car. In fact, one day
as I was backing out oh so carefully, I got too close on the *other*
side and hit my driver side mirror against the garage. It was a
minor accident, but how embarrassing! With the glass cracked
and the housing bent out of shape, there was no disguising
what had happened; the part would need to be replaced.

When I rather sheepishly explained what had happened to
our dealer, he just laughed and said, "Think nothing of it. These
town house garages are so narrow, there's a lady who has come
in here three times for the same thing!" I laughed with him, but
added all the same: "I won't be back. If I do it again, I'll be so
embarrassed I'll have to go somewhere else!"

Paying attention is critical in so many areas of life, whether
it's backing out of the garage, tending to friendships, listening
in class, taking care of our health, playing a sport, nurturing our
marriage, working, parenting, or anything else. And just as I
paid attention to one side of my car at the expense of the other,

I realize that my attention can get lopsided in more important ways too. Sometimes I pay more attention to my work at the expense of my personal life. Or I focus my attention outward and neglect my inward life. I need to pay attention not just in the different areas of my life—like the different pieces of a giant jigsaw puzzle—but in the larger sense of paying attention to God and to the whole puzzle picture of my life. Instead of assorted fragments pulling my attention in various ways, I long for wholeness.

Let the words of my mouth and the meditation of my heart be acceptable to you, O Lord, my rock and my redeemer (Psalm 19:14).

Moment by moment

One way of cultivating this kind of attention is described by Frank Laubach in his "Game with Minutes." The goal is to remember God for at least one second out of every minute for a whole hour. He suggests playing the game in church, on the way home, at mealtimes, when walking alone, in the middle of a busy Monday morning. Laubach calls it a game, "because it is a delightful experience and an exhilarating spiritual exercise."[1] It's not meant to be a chore, but a wonderful discovery and a delight.

While Frank Laubach is perhaps better known as a missionary to the Philippines and a pioneer in literacy training around the world, he clearly also paid attention to his inner life. The game he proposed was for an hour, but the intent went far beyond that, to sustained attention on God throughout the day. Just as Jesus' first disciples were with him day and night for three years, just as Enoch "walked with God,"[2] just as Brother Lawrence practiced the presence of God as he went about his

---

1. Frank C. Laubach, *The Game with Minutes*, (1953), 2.
2. Genesis 5:24.

daily tasks, so Frank Laubach's game was also meant to be an exercise in paying attention, to bring the whole of life into focus with God.

One congregation tried it during their regular worship, with each person being given their own scorecard. In explaining the game, the pastor asked the congregation to think about God at least once each minute and to keep score by recording the number of successful minutes. At the end of the hour-long service, the tally showed scores from 5 minutes to 60 minutes, with an average of 44 minutes, or 73 percent.

I thought I might try this with my own congregation some Sunday morning, to see how focused on God we might become in our own worship time. But as I thought more about how we might do this, I wondered if it would even be possible to keep score. Did Frank Laubach's congregation have a clock in their sanctuary, or did everyone have their own watch? Did they simply "guesstimate" each minute and the degree of their attention? Wouldn't their attempts to track their time for every minute take away from their attention to God? I decided it wouldn't work to do it with my congregation after all.

When I try the Game with Minutes myself, I don't actually time each minute, and it's not always for an hour. I seldom wear a watch and don't want to be checking my wall clock or cell phone every minute. For me, watching the clock and setting a time limit would defeat the purpose. To be honest, I don't actually keep score either, so I suppose my version of the game is not really a game at all, but a less structured personal exercise.

In my version, I simply try to be mindful of God for as much of the time as I can. I find it easiest in Sunday morning worship where there is so much that recalls me to God each minute: the words of a song, a prayer, the reading of Scripture, my sermon. It's a little harder while I prepare supper, but still I can turn my attention to God even then. As I measure out the rice, I am thankful for God's provision and pray for those who are without food today. As I slice carrots and celery, I pray for the guests who will join us for supper. I pray for an awareness of God's presence among us. Just as in Laubach's original Game with Minutes, my thoughts may not be focused on God every second (was that a teaspoon of cumin, or half a teaspoon? I'd better check my recipe), but with practice I become more deliberately aware than before.

Abide in me as I abide in you. Just as the branch cannot bear fruit by itself unless it abides in the vine, neither can you unless you abide in me. I am the vine, you are the branches (John 15:4-5).

The thing I like best about this practice is how it enlarges my vision and prevents me from getting too narrowly focused on whatever it is I'm doing at the moment. So instead of obsessively cleaning the house because company's coming or agonizing over a sermon that just doesn't seem to be coming together, I can lift my eyes from my task and rest in God's presence. The most important thing is not having the house in order or preparing the perfect meal, but that God is our host, bringing us together. The most important thing is not that a sermon goes the way I think it ought to go, but that I place myself and my sermon in God's hands.

Just that shift of turning my attention away from myself and toward God gives me a break from my immediate concerns—a moment-by-moment sense of God's presence, anywhere, anytime, if the game is played Laubach's way. Instead of focusing on just one narrow area of life, I lift my eyes from my own concerns to the breadth of God's work and will in all my life and in the world around me. In the light of God's constant presence and care, my burdens lift, the fragmented pieces of my life come together, and I see my life whole.

Life review

Another exercise in paying attention is the examen of consciousness, which is part of *The Spiritual Exercises of St. Ignatius of Loyola.*[3] The examen is a methodical way of paying attention to one's life and bringing it to God in prayer. When done first thing in the morning, it's a good way to begin the day with thanksgiving to God. Practiced at midday or evening, it serves as a review of whatever has happened to that point. *The Exercises* outline five basic parts to the examen:

1. Give thanks to God.
2. Ask for God's grace in reviewing one's life.
3. Review one's life hour by hour.
4. Ask God's pardon for faults.
5. Receive God's grace for moving forward.

Although my copy of *The Spiritual Exercises* calls this an examen of "conscience," most today refer to it as an examen of "consciousness" to emphasize that the examen is not narrowly focused on sin and examining one's conscience, but on the larger sense of being conscious of God in the whole of life. As well, today there are many variations of the examen. Some follow the original five movements outlined in *The Spiritual Exercises*, some offer lists of many more questions, some seem to use the term *examen* to mean any kind of reflection and review of one's life.

For me, the examen of consciousness has been most helpful at night as a way of looking back on my day—not just thinking through the who-what-where-why-when of everything that's happened, but reflecting also on my thoughts and feelings, my sense of God's presence or absence, when I've been tired or where I've felt a special energy, the gifts I've received,

Journal Prompt

Reread your journal entries to this point. Where do you see God at work in your life? Where do you see continued need for healing? Give thanks for all God's gifts, and receive God's mercy.

---

3. St. Ignatius of Loyola, *The Spiritual Exercises of St. Ignatius of Loyola*, Father Elder Mullan, tr. (New York: P.J. Kenedy & Sons, 1914), "First Week: Method for Making the General Examen." Christian Classics Ethereal Library, http://www.ccel.org/ccel/ignatius/exercises.pdf.

the lessons that I've learned throughout the day. It's a way of paying attention both to my life as a whole and to how God has been present and at work within it. Phyllis Zagano's five-part outline and Scripture references have been especially helpful and are used here with permission, along with my own examples and reflection:[4]

1. Recall you are in the presence of God.

In *The Spiritual Exercises*, the General Examen begins with giving thanks, but here Zagano takes a helpful step back, so I can first collect myself and my thoughts in the presence of God. As she points out from the apostle Paul's speech to a crowd in Athens, "In [God] we live and move and have our being."[5] That's always true but not always apparent in the way we live, so I appreciate starting my examen with this reminder.

2. Look at your day with gratitude.

For me, this is usually easy. I'm thankful for waking up each day, most often early without an alarm clock; for the way the sky gradually lightens even on a cloudy day; for emails from all my sisters; the wave from a neighbor; a gifted congregation and ministry team; my husband's turn to cook; my nephew getting his cast off; God loving me no matter what. As Mary the mother of Jesus says, "My soul magnifies the Lord. . . . for the Mighty One has done great things for me, and holy is his name."[6] I'm thankful for all of God's gifts both great and small.

3. Ask help from the Holy Spirit.

Before reviewing my life, I ask for God's help, for as Jesus said to his disciples, "When the Spirit of truth comes, he will guide you into all the truth."[7] That's what I hope for as I spend

---

4. Phyllis Zagano, "Examen of Consciousness: Finding God in All Things," *Catholic Update*, St. Anthony Messenger Press/Franciscan Media, March 2003. Used with permission.
5. Acts 17:28.
6. Luke 1:46b, 49.
7. John 16:13.

time paying attention and reflecting on my day—that the Holy Spirit will open my eyes to the daily joys, gifts, doubts, weaknesses, and other aspects of my life and cover them all with God's mercy.

4. Review your day.

If an evening examen takes about twenty minutes, I might spend twelve to fifteen minutes on just this one step. This is the time to mentally walk through the events of the day, reflecting on my thoughts, feelings, attitudes, and habits. Was I kind? Was I too quick to judge? Did I speak when I should have been silent? Or was I silent when I should have said something? What were the reasons for my behavior? Where was I especially aware of God in my day?

For those given to too much introspection and self-reproach, it may be wise to consider a time limit for this section, and/or to focus on questions in pairs that provide some natural balance. Where did I feel most alive/least alive with God's Spirit today? What made me the happiest/saddest? This is not meant as an exercise in negativity but an exercise of positive discovery. "Examine yourselves to see whether you are living in the faith. Test yourselves. Do you not realize that Jesus Christ is in you?"[8]

5. Reconcile and resolve.

As I reflect on my day, I may become aware of places where I need forgiveness and healing, places where I have wounded someone else or have been wounded by others. It may not be possible to reconcile and resolve every situation immediately, but I can receive God's grace and allow it to work within me even now. As the Lord says to the prophet, I am "just like the clay in the potter's hand."[9] So where there is sorrow and brokenness in my day, I claim the words of the psalmist that God "heals

---

8. 2 Corinthians 13:5.
9. Jeremiah 18:6.

the brokenhearted, and binds up their wounds."[10] Where there is joy in my day, "I rejoice in the LORD."[11] I place my trust in God to shape and reshape me as I look forward with hope.

In *The Spiritual Exercises*, the General Examen ends with the Lord's Prayer, which draws the time of prayer and reflection to a close. "Our Father" is the one in whom I live and move and have my being. I am thankful to God who gives me "daily bread" and all the other things on my gratitude list. I can rely on God in every part of my day for "yours is the power and the glory, forever and ever. Amen."

Sacred pause: focus your attention

What helps you to be fully present at any given moment? How do you focus your attention? Try one or more of the following options as your spiritual practice for today:

(1) Choose an hour during the course of your day to try the Game with Minutes. Don't worry about timing each minute exactly, but simply turn your attention to God as you go about your daily tasks. At the end of the hour, consider your approximate score. Are you surprised? Disappointed? Challenged to try again? Reflect on your experience in your journal. Choose another hour on a different day, and compare your two experiences.

(2) Set aside some time in the evening to review your day. Begin by remembering God's love and care for you; there is nothing to fear. Ask for God's help as you allow the day to unfold in your mind's eye. Where is there joy and blessing? Give thanks. Where is there pain and need for healing? Receive God's mercy. How were you drawn to God today? How did you express God's love to others? End your reflection by praying the Lord's Prayer.

---

10. Psalm 147:3.
11. Psalm 104:34.

(3) Consider your life until this moment, and list seven significant events in your journal. It may be a milestone moment like getting your first job or celebrating your wedding, or it may be a recurring theme like playing Little League or going camping every summer as a family. It may be something to celebrate or a difficult time like the death of a loved one. Perhaps it's some other kind of turning point that may seem quite ordinary to others but is significant to you. As you look back, how was God present in each event? Where is there still need for healing? What did you learn about God? End your reflection by praying the Lord's Prayer.

15

Confessing

I said, "I will confess my transgressions to the LORD,"
and you forgave the guilt of my sin.
Psalm 32:5

In the fourth century, St. Augustine wrote the story of his con-
version to Christian faith and called it *Confessions*. With a title
like that, we might well expect it to be an intimate look at his
private life, perhaps revealing some things that might not quite
fit his later reputation as an influential leader and theologian of
the early church. That's why I wasn't exactly surprised to read that
as a young man St. Augustine took a mistress who gave birth to
his son, and then how he finally came to faith and was baptized.

The basic meaning of confession is simply "to own or to
acknowledge the truth." For St. Augustine that meant beginning his autobiography with words of praise to God: "Great art
Thou, O Lord, and greatly to be praised; great is Thy power,
and Thy wisdom infinite."[1] Owning the truth also meant
recalling the "carnal corruptions" of his soul, "not because I love
them, but that I may love Thee, O my God."[2] Confession of sin
was also part of St. Augustine's truth, and part of his genuine
relationship with God.

---

1. St. Augustine, *The Confessions of St. Augustine*, Edward B. Pusey, tr., date unknown, Book I, Chapter I. Christian Classics Ethereal Library, http://www.ccel.org/
ccel/augustine/confess.pdf.
2. St. Augustine, *The Confessions of St. Augustine*, Edward B. Pusey, tr., date unknown, Book II, Chapter I. Christian Classics Ethereal Library, http://www.ccel.org/
ccel/augustine/confess.pdf.

As I come to God with the truth of my own life, I realize that I also come with sin and brokenness. No flagrant infidelities or anything that would appear on a police report, but at times I'm willful, impatient, thoughtless, selfish, wasteful. If all my sins were placed on my back, they would be too heavy to bear, and that's the truth for all humanity.

But praise be to God through Jesus Christ who has borne all our sins away by his life, death, and resurrection. Because of Jesus, confession is not simply browbeating ourselves for our failures. Confession is release from guilt. Confession is freedom and a fresh start. Confession is part of a genuine relationship with God.

Confessing sin

I understand why the examen of "conscience" in *The Spiritual Exercises* is now more commonly called the examen of "consciousness," to highlight a broader awareness of God's presence in our lives. And yet it seems to me that St. Ignatius really did mean "conscience" in the narrower sense of examining ourselves for sin. After all, he describes the second point of the General Examen "to ask grace to know our sins and cast them out," the fourth point "to ask pardon," and the fifth "to purpose amendment with His grace."[3] Clearly this examen includes the awareness of our own frailty and sin as part of our broader awareness of God's presence in our lives. Next to the holiness and greatness of God, we all falter.

During and immediately after the Stanley Cup riots in Vancouver, some people were saying that it was caused by hooligans, by troublemakers, by people who weren't even hockey fans. But later, as those responsible began to own up to the truth about the looting and setting vehicles on fire, people

---

3. St. Ignatius of Loyola, *The Spiritual Exercises of St. Ignatius of Loyola*, Father Elder Mullan, tr., (New York: P.J. Kenedy & Sons, 1914). Christian Classics Ethereal Library, http://www.ccel.org/ccel/ignatius/exercises.pdf, 29.

realized that yes, they were actually fans, and they were good people, including a star athlete and honor roll student. Yet, at the same time, they were also people who had said and done the wrong things and later regretted their behavior.

Both sins of commission and sins of omission were part of the Anglican confession that I learned as a teenager: "We have left undone those things which we ought to have done; and we have done those things which we ought not to have done." We might not be guilty of setting a car on fire or taunting the police or a hundred other things we might think of, but we have all left some things undone that we should have done, and we have all done things which we should not have done.

Unlike St. Augustine in the fourth century or St. Ignatius in the sixteenth century, today we are much more likely to talk about failures, mistakes, or poor judgment instead of sin. After all, anyone can make a mistake or take a wrong turn. Anyone can have a weak moment. That's not really so bad, is it? But however much we may minimize or explain away sin, the truth is that we all do it. As a letter to the early church puts it, "If we say that we have no sin, we deceive ourselves, and the truth is not in us."[4]

Confession means owning up to the truth of that. Sometimes we may be forced into it because we get found out, as some of the Stanley Cup rioters were found out on Facebook. But at its best, confession comes from personal conviction and a desire to come

> **One way of defining *sin* is by using the Ten Commandments:**
> You shall have no other gods before me.
> You shall not make for yourself an idol.
> You shall not make wrongful use of the name of the LORD your God.
> Remember the sabbath day and keep it holy.
> Honor your father and your mother.
> You shall not murder.
> You shall not commit adultery.
> You shall not steal.
> You shall not bear false witness.
> You shall not covet
> (Exodus 20:1-17, summarized).

---

4. 1 John 1:8.

clean. Then "[i]f we confess our sins, he who is faithful and just will forgive us our sins and cleanse us from all unrighteousness."[5]

Psalm 32 is a good illustration of this, as it first describes the psalmist's personal experience with unconfessed sin: "While I kept silence, my body wasted away through my groaning all day long." His guilty conscience was a great burden to him, and when he could no longer bear it, he found that the solution was actually quite simple: "Then I acknowledged my sin to you, and I did not hide my iniquity; I said, 'I will confess my transgressions to the LORD,' and you forgave the guilt of my sin."[6] The psalmist confessed, and God forgave.

Is it really that simple? At times, we may act as if it's much more complicated: I confessed, I felt terrible for years on end, I told myself I would never amount to anything, I took it out on my spouse and kids, and never really got over it anyway—and then God forgave me. Or sometimes we may try to deny any sense of wrongdoing and bury our feelings in overwork, overeating, overexercising, or other excess.

How ironic all of this is, since God already knows all about us! Besides, as Richard Foster writes, "at the heart of God is the desire to forgive and to give. Because of this He set into motion the entire redemptive process that culminated in the cross and was confirmed in the resurrection."[7] It's really that simple. Through the work of God in Jesus Christ, we have forgiveness from sin and the power to live a new life.

Living beyond confession

In 1988, when Canadian Prime Minister Brian Mulroney apologized for the internment of Japanese Canadians during the Second World War, he said, "Apologies are the only way we

---

5. 1 John 1:9.
6. Psalm 32:1-5.
7. Richard Foster, *Celebration of Discipline: The Path to Spiritual Growth* (San Francisco: Harper & Row, 1978), 125.

can cleanse the past."[8] Certainly, an apology is a good start as we acknowledge the truth, but true confession is not only about acknowledging the past, it's also about the way we live in the present and future. Confession may start with an apology, but it also involves repentance and making things right; it leads to a new relationship with God and with other people; it means moving beyond the apology to living a new life.

Confession means accepting the consequences of our behavior. Consider the man who embezzled funds from his employer. Although he was deeply sorry, paid back the money, and was able to avoid criminal charges, he also resigned from his position. A student confessed to plagiarizing his paper, but he still received a zero on that assignment. A woman spread gossip and betrayed a friend, and although she has expressed her regret, the break in their relationship is still healing, and it will take time for trust to be rebuilt. Confession cannot change the past, but it means doing what we can to make amends: to repay the money we've stolen, to end the inappropriate relationship, to stop lying, or whatever it is we need to do.

Journal Prompt

Think of a time when you offered an apology to someone. Did you make amends in some other way as well? What was their response? Or, think of a time when someone apologized to you. Did they make amends in some other way as well? How did you receive their apology? Imagine yourself back in one of these situations. How did you feel? What did you say? Would you do anything different?

One day when Jesus was teaching at the temple, the scribes and Pharisees came to him with a woman who had been "caught in the very act of committing adultery." It was hardly a confession—an accusation really—since the scribes and Pharisees were doing all the talking: "Now in the law Moses commanded us to stone such women. Now what do you say?" After a moment,

8. Mitch Miyagawa, "A Sorry State" in *Cultivating Canada: Reconciliation through the Lens of Cultural Diversity* (Ottawa: Aboriginal Healing Foundation, 2011), 353.

Jesus replied, "Let anyone among you who is without sin be the first to throw a stone at her." He didn't deny their accusation of her sin, but he just as surely turned their accusation back against them. Why were they so concerned about this woman and so unconcerned about their own sin? Why did they seize her alone and not the man who had been with her? One by one, the men slipped away, and Jesus finally said to the woman, "Neither do I condemn you. Go your way, and from now on do not sin again."[9]

> Create in me a clean heart, O God,
> and put a new and right spirit within me.
> Do not cast me away from your presence,
> and do not take your holy spirit from me.
> Restore to me the joy of your salvation,
> and sustain in me a willing spirit (Psalm 51:10-12).

Jesus did not condemn the woman, but he clearly called her to a new way of living. She was not to continue as before; instead, she was to move beyond her past into a new present and new future, transformed by God's forgiveness in Jesus Christ. Old Testament scholar and theologian Walter Brueggemann says, "The lucky ones are not those free of transgression, but those able to move beyond it."[10] As Psalm 51 describes, there is joy in being forgiven and living a new life.[11]

But what about those times when we can't seem to move on, when we seem stuck in some feedback loop and can't break free to live that new life? What about those things that seem so persistent and deeply engrained—like that streak of jealousy that prevents us from truly celebrating a friend's achievement? Or that spirit of wanting more and more that makes us want to buy everything in the store? Or the way those of us in North America consume far more than our fair share of resources and

---

9. John 8:2-11.
10. Walter Brueggemann, *The Message of the Psalms* (Minneapolis: Augsburg Publishing House, 1984), 95.
11. Psalm 51:11-12.

whose governments go to great lengths to keep it that way? What does confession mean when we seem to encounter the same temptations and make the same mistakes again and again? What does confession mean when we continue to be part of larger political and social structures of injustice?

I just can't seem to repent and move beyond these things once and for all. I need confession again and again, because confession is not only for the sins that we do or don't do. Confession also means acknowledging our inner dispositions: the unkind thoughts that spring up unbidden, the secret grudge, the lust for what we can't or shouldn't have. Confession also means acknowledging our role as part of a much larger historical, political, social, and economic context. Even if I do what I can to avoid certain companies, or choose to pay more for fairly traded coffee, or look harder for the nontoxic carpet cleaner, I remain enmeshed in a system that is riddled with greed, abuse, oppression, and violence. That too is part of my confession.

Owning up to all of this takes humility. Like the apostle Paul, I can't seem to do all of the good things that I want to do, and at the same time I seem to keep on doing the bad things that I want to stop. Paul's personal struggle became so intense that he cried out, "Wretched man that I am! Who will rescue me from this body of death?" Paul knew that he could not solve his problem on his own. But the answer came to him immediately, "Thanks be to God through Jesus Christ our Lord!"[12] In confession, I too realize that I cannot solve the problem of sin on my own, but like Paul, I can turn to God in Jesus Christ with humility and thanks.

Sacred pause: practice confession

Take some time for reflection and listening to God with one of the following options. If you have a tendency to blame and berate yourself for not being perfect, take care not to get stuck

---

12. Romans 7:24-25.

in a rut of feeling guilty. Allow God to move you into the joy of being forgiven.

(1) As you become quiet, is there some situation or relationship in need of confession that comes to mind? Do you need to make an apology? Do you need to repent and change your attitude or behavior? Is there something that you need to do to make amends? Make your confession to God, and seek God's guidance on what you need to do next. Can you write a note, make a phone call, or make amends in some other way? Be sincere, and in humility, leave the results to God.

> Jesus' greatest commandment: You shall love the Lord your God with all your heart, and with all your soul, and with all your mind. You shall love your neighbor as yourself (Matthew 22:37-39, summarized).

(2) Use the Ten Commandments or Jesus' greatest commandment to reflect on your life. Where have you fallen short? Make your confession to God, and receive the assurance of forgiveness: "Bless the LORD, O my soul, and all that is within me, bless his holy name. Bless the LORD, O my soul, and do not forget all his benefits—who forgives all your iniquity, who heals all your diseases, who redeems your life from the Pit, who crowns you with steadfast love and mercy, who satisfies you with good as long as you live so that your youth is renewed like the eagle's."[13]

(3) Psalm 51 speaks of the joy of being forgiven. Does that describe your present experience? Can you recall a time when you did feel that way? What are some of the barriers that might keep you from experiencing the joy of being forgiven?

13. Psalm 103:1-5.

16

Praying Scripture

The unfolding of your words gives light.
Psalm 119:130

When I read the Saturday morning newspaper, I generally scan all the headlines; stop to read any articles of particular interest; work through the *New York Times* crossword puzzle; skim the comics and finish the Sudoku in the upper right corner of the same page; look through the business section but skip the stock reports; flip through the travel section; glance at the sports; ignore the classifieds. My "reading" is actually a combination of several different things—scanning for information or interest, reading for entertainment or relaxation, paying attention to some parts and ignoring others. The way I read, a single newspaper can last the entire weekend!

We may also read Scripture for different reasons and in different ways: for information or historical background, for the sake of a good story or inspiring poetry, for Bible study or spiritual growth. We may focus on certain parts of the Bible and skip over others. We may read whole books, or shorter sections, or just a single verse here and there. The way we read depends a great deal on our purpose.

Praying Scripture is another way of reading and understanding the Bible. In this form of reading, the purpose is not to skim quickly for information, but to read slowly and to pay close attention to the text, to read for spiritual refreshment and discernment. As a way of praying, its focus is not on the words we speak to God, but on becoming attentive to the word that God will speak to us. In praying Scripture, we seek "to go beyond information to formation—to being formed and molded by what we read. We are listening with the heart to the Holy within. This prayerful reading, as we might call it, transforms us and strengthens us."[1]

Lectio divina

Lectio divina is one way of praying Scripture. Literally a "divine reading," this is an ancient practice with roots in Jewish contemplative reading and a long tradition in Christian monastic spirituality. In its contemporary form, the steps of *lectio divina* are often named and described in different ways,[2] using different texts of Scripture, practiced alone or in small group settings or even as an entire congregation. There is a richness to the practice of *lectio divina*, but in all its variations, it brings together a number of spiritual disciplines that all have their part to play: slowing down, silence, reading Scripture, prayer, simplicity.

For me, *lectio divina* does not in fact begin with *lectio*—with the reading of Scripture—but first of all with *silencio*. This silence is a time of preparation, a time to become quiet, a time to set aside the concerns of the day, to turn my thoughts *to* God in expectation of hearing *from* God. I choose a Scripture text—a psalm, a story, a paragraph of a letter, perhaps no more than fifteen verses. Then *lectio* is reading the text slowly and prayerfully, allowing each word to have its full weight. In the ancient world, reading was always aloud, so I try to read the text aloud as well, listening for God to focus my attention on one particular word or phrase.

1. Richard J. Foster and James Bryan Smith, eds., *Devotional Classics: Selected Readings for Individuals and Groups* (San Francisco: HarperSanFrancisco, 1993), 2–3.
2. See, for example, Ruth Haley Barton, *Sacred Rhythms* (Downers Grove: IVP Books, 2006), 54–61, and Tony Jones, *Soul Shaper* (Grand Rapids: Zondervan, 2003), 36–45, for youth ministry.

In *meditatio*, I read the Scripture once more, asking God to show me how this particular word or phrase might connect with my life in a specific way. *Oratio* is a third reading and a time for me to respond with prayer and with words of my own offered back to God.

Then I rest before God in *contemplatio*, holding the word or phrase in contemplation and letting it sink in more deeply. Finally, I end with *incarnatio*—a resolve to let this word continue with me throughout the day and to live it out.

Described step by step, *lectio divina* may seem rather artificial and rigid, mechanical even. How can God speak through such a stilted process? Yet, with practice, I find the steps of *lectio divina* actually come quite naturally. One flows into another as I find my rhythm with God, and I am amazed again and again at the way God speaks through such a simple practice.

Journal Prompt

If you are already familiar with *lectio divina*, describe the steps in your own words. How do they compare with the version described in this chapter? What has been the value of *lectio divina* for you? If this is new to you, consider the difference between reading the newspaper and reading Scripture. What makes reading "sacred"?

Yesterday, I took a few moments for *lectio divina* as my afternoon "coffee break." Instead of my usual New Revised Standard Version, I took the Common English Bible, since it's a more recent translation and less familiar to me. After *silencio*, a moment of silence, I turned to the narrative of Lydia's faith story in Acts 16:11-15.

My first try at *lectio* seemed unfocused, even though I tried to concentrate as I read aloud. I found myself latching on to different words and phrases: the side of the river described as "a place of prayer," how Lydia was a "God-worshiper," how she came to "embrace" Paul's message. Everything jumped out at me, and I found myself skipping from one word or phrase to another, unable to settle on anything for long.

I paused for silence once more and tried again, *lectio*. The second time through, I read even more slowly, more attentively. This time just one phrase seemed to stand out, a phrase that I all but missed the first time: "the Lord enabled her."

As I moved on to *meditatio*, my attention was drawn even more closely to the first part of the phrase "*the Lord* enabled her." It was the Lord that opened Lydia's ears to receive Paul's message, the Lord that confirmed it in her heart. So too it was the Lord that enabled me.

Oratio came almost immediately and like a flood. I responded with thanks that I did not need to rely on my own strength; I realized how often I had acted without such a firm sense of God's enabling; I felt a sense of relief as the tasks of the day seemed to shrink to a more manageable size and fall into place. My day did not depend on my own abilities or disabilities, but on *the Lord* who enabled me. I rested with that thought in *contemplatio* before moving on with the rest of my day.

When I was ready, part of my *incarnatio* was to personalize the phrase and put it in the present tense for myself. My *lectio divina* "coffee break" was over. But the word of God revealed during that time continued with me through the rest of the day. In prayer for those in crisis who must bear unbearable suffering, the Lord enables me. Wrestling with Scripture and sermon, the

---

Scripture for lectio divina

To start, I find that passages of Scripture from several verses up to fifteen verses in length are the most manageable. A single verse might not give enough context, and much longer passages may be more difficult to sustain good attention.

If the text is a familiar one, you may find it helpful to try a less familiar translation, but I find that even a familiar text in a familiar

translation may yield new insight. Allow God to guide your choice of text, and read with expectation. Here are some places to start:
> **Psalm 19**
> **Psalm 121**
> **Isaiah 40:28-31**
> **Lamentations 3:21-26**
> **Matthew 6:25-34**
> **Mark 10:46-52**
> **John 14:1-14**
> **Romans 12:1-2**
> **1 Corinthians 13**

Lord enables me. Having tea with a friend in tears and needing a word of hope, the Lord enables me. Whatever the task or challenge for the rest of the day, the Lord enables me.

Each experience with *lectio divina* is different. As I pray through different texts, I expect to hear from God with a word of help, teaching, encouragement, comfort, challenge, forgiveness, direction, or in some other way. Is it like that every time? No, of course not. At times I may be too tired to concentrate, or *lectio divina* just doesn't seem to "work" for some unknown reason. At those times when I feel as if God has nothing to say to me or perhaps I just can't hear, I simply spend the few moments in quiet or go on to something else. I can try *lectio divina* again some other time.

Sometimes meeting in a group is helpful when the combined energy of others helps me focus. At other times, I may become impatient with the sharing time that is part of the group process, for when I have begun to focus, we break for sharing, and just as I have managed to refocus once again, there's another sharing time. Impatience may count these as "interruptions," but if I am willing, they can also be wonderful opportunities to learn from others and to hear from God through them.

The Jesus Prayer

Another form of praying Scripture is simply to pray using the words of Scripture. Praying the Lord's Prayer is perhaps one of the most well-known examples of this. But other, shorter prayers from Scripture may be used throughout the day as a kind of refrain to return to again and again: "To you, O Lord, I lift up my soul."[3] "Have mercy on me, O God."[4] Repeating such brief prayers over and over throughout the day is one way to "persevere in prayer"[5] and to "pray without ceasing."[6]

---

3. Psalm 25:1.
4. Psalm 51:1.
5. Romans 12:12.
6. 1 Thessalonians 5:17.

Breathe in—"To you, O Lord"—Breathe out—"I lift up my soul." Breathe in—"To you, O Lord"—Breathe out—"I lift up my soul." It's simple enough to do at any time, anywhere, when spending time alone with God or going about one's daily tasks: preparing meals, eating, walking, working. Each breath can be a prayer. Breathe in—"To you, O Lord"—Breathe out—"I lift up my soul." Breathe in—"To you, O Lord"—Breathe out—"I lift up my soul."

As creatures that need oxygen to live, we breathe automatically and unconsciously. With every breath, we depend on God's Spirit who sustains the world. How fitting then, to link our prayers to the rhythm of our breathing. Breath prayers remind us that we depend on God as much as we depend on the air that we breathe. Breath prayers remind us that we need to pray. They engage both mind and body, both heart and soul. With each breath, we pray with our whole being.

In the Eastern Orthodox Church, the Jesus Prayer is a simple and profound breath prayer: "Lord Jesus Christ, Son of God, have mercy on me, a sinner." Breathe in—"Lord Jesus Christ, Son of God"—Breathe out—"have mercy on me, a sinner." The words are drawn from Scripture, from one of Jesus' parables about a tax collector who prays, "God, be merciful to me, a sinner!"[7] and from a blind man who calls out to the Lord, "Jesus, Son of David, have mercy on me!"[8] Even though the crowds tell the man to be quiet, he calls out again, "Son of David, have mercy on me!" Jesus hears the man's cries, calls him out of the crowd, asks him what he wants, and responds by restoring his sight.

While the words of the Jesus Prayer can be identified with these two stories, the prayer is even more broadly grounded in Scripture. "Lord Jesus Christ" is the Lord of all things,[9] the One

7. Luke 18:13.
8. Luke 18:35-43.
9. Colossians 1:15-18.

born to bring salvation,[10] the Chosen (literally anointed) One.[11] "Son of God" is the One who is fully divine yet fully human, who knew hunger, thirst, temptation, sorrow, suffering, humiliation, even death, and yet was without sin.[12] "Have mercy on me, a sinner" acknowledges our weakness and failure and asks for God's forgiveness, mercy, and help.[13] Each phrase is rich with meaning, and this brief prayer "contains a whole theology."[14]

In *Mysteries of the Jesus Prayer*, author and producer/director Norris J. Chumley describes his eight years of research for a documentary on the Jesus Prayer. His work takes him to monasteries in Egypt, Russia, Ukraine, and Greece to interview monks and nuns on their spiritual practice. He clearly admires those who live out their calling to a monastic vocation, but he is also convinced "that the Jesus Prayer can be a useful tool for anyone seeking a deeper spiritual life. . . . It can enrich the life of anyone who prays it faithfully and with concentration. The point is to add prayer into your existing routine, not to change your lifestyle in order to become a monk, or monklike."[15]

I often pray a shorter form of the prayer, simply: "Lord Jesus Christ, have mercy." I pray it for myself, and I pray it for others. For the friend who looks so together on the outside, but who secretly struggles with depression—"Lord Jesus Christ, have mercy." For the couple who started out as friends and now after years of marriage look at each other as strangers—"Lord Jesus Christ, have mercy." For those who are going hungry today, starving today, while others have too much—"Lord Jesus Christ, have mercy." For when I don't know how to pray for

10. Matthew 1:21.
11. Luke 9:28-35.
12. Hebrews 4:15.
13. Psalm 51:1; Psalm 109:26; Matthew 15:25; Luke 17:12-19.
14. Norris J. Chumley, *Mysteries of the Jesus Prayer: Experiencing the Presence of God and a Pilgrimage to the Heart of an Ancient Spirituality* (New York: HarperCollins, 2011), 21ff.
15. Ibid., 19.

someone I care about, for when I don't know what to pray for a situation that seems to have no solution—"Lord Jesus Christ, have mercy."

Sacred pause: pray with Scripture

For your spiritual practice today, try *lectio divina* and/or praying the Jesus Prayer, and then reflect on your experience:

(1) For *lectio divina*, read Acts 16:11-15 as I did, or another portion of Scripture. Allow God to move you naturally through the steps from silence to reading, from reflection to living out the word that is revealed to you. In praying Scripture, turn your thoughts from your own concerns to the text, listen for God's leading and teaching, and allow God to bring you back full circle to your daily life.

(2) For the Jesus Prayer, begin by finding a quiet spot where you can be alone with God. Stand, sit, or lie quietly, relaxing your mind and body by quietly breathing in and out. Then when you are ready, silently repeat the prayer "Lord Jesus Christ, Son of God, have mercy on me, a sinner." Say this prayer each time you breathe, inhaling on "Lord Jesus Christ, Son of God," and exhaling on "have mercy on me, a sinner." Rest in the words

---

As an alternative, try praying one of the following short prayers from Scripture. Like the Jesus Prayer, these prayer sentences may be used as breath prayers during a quiet time alone with God or throughout your day.

• Show me your glory, I pray (Exodus 33:18).
• O give thanks to the LORD, for he is good; for his steadfast love endures forever (1 Chronicles 16:34).
• To you, O LORD, I lift up my soul (Psalm 25:1).

• Make me to know your ways, O LORD; teach me your paths (Psalm 25:4).
• In you, O LORD, I seek refuge (Psalm 31:1).
• Have mercy on me, O God, according to your steadfast love (Psalm 51:1).
• Jesus, Son of David, have mercy on me (Mark 10:47).
• I thank my God through Jesus Christ (Romans 1:8).
• Hallelujah! For the Lord our God the Almighty reigns (Revelation 19:6).

as you pray. If your mind wanders, gently bring it back. Allow God's Spirit to guide you.

(3) Reflect on your experience with *lectio divina* and/or the Jesus Prayer in your journal. Do you find it difficult to become still? Are you able to focus, or do you find yourself becoming distracted or bored? How does your experience with *lectio divina* change as you practice it with different texts of Scripture? How does your experience with the Jesus Prayer change throughout the day?

Remember that even when these practices may not seem to "work," even when our prayers seem to fall flat, we can be assured that God is at work, for "the Spirit helps us in our weakness; for we do not know how to pray as we ought, but that very Spirit intercedes with sighs too deep for words."[16]

---

16. Romans 8:26.

17

Living Simply

One thing I asked of the LORD,
that will I seek after.
Psalm 27:4

As a young married couple, my husband and I flew to Elkhart, Indiana, to begin seminary studies. We took four large cardboard boxes, a carry-on bag, and a "transportable" computer that would just fit under an airline seat. We traveled light both by necessity and by choice. By necessity, because airline regulations limited the amount of baggage. By choice, because—with the exception of the computer—we were trying to live as simply as we knew how. The small city of Elkhart was not exactly the Walden Woods of Henry David Thoreau, but in our own way, we wanted to "live deliberately"[1] and to experiment with our own version of the simple life.

Since we were to live in furnished housing at the seminary, we took only the essentials: clothing, linens, dishes, a few books packed tightly into the cardboard boxes, the computer, and a small bag for personal items. We flew to Indiana because we had not owned a car for several years, and once in Elkhart, we got around on foot and by bus. No television at home. No microwave. No prepackaged foods. No dishwasher but our own hands.

As time went on, we added to our household. We wrote home and had a few more things sent to us by mail: my

---

1. Henry D. Thoreau, *Walden* (Princeton: Princeton University Press, 1973), 90.

husband's suit that he didn't think he'd need, a few more books, and dishes. In Elkhart, we bought another blanket (winter was colder than we thought) and another pot so we could cook for friends. But mostly we made do. The seminary provided our small one-bedroom apartment furnished with the basics. The public library supplied the artwork that brightened our walls.

Now years later, our lives have changed. In some ways, we still live more simply than many people around us. ("How can you live without a microwave?" I was asked just last week.) I still walk to the produce store when I have time. I still cook mainly with whole foods. The public library is still one of my favorite—and least expensive—forms of entertainment. But now my husband and I live in our own townhouse with two floors, three bedrooms, and three bathrooms. There is a dishwasher, courtesy of the previous owners. We have a television and a PVR, a double garage and two cars. We have shelves of books at home, in my study at the church, and in my husband's office at the college where he teaches.

Journal Prompt

On a scale from 1 (least simple) to 5 (most simple), how would you rate your current way of life? How has this changed over the years, if at all? Is living a simple life important to you? Why or why not?

Most people say that we have done well, that we have come a long way from our days as students. They say, "You've worked hard." They say, "You deserve it." But as for me, I miss the woman who could pack her belongings in four cardboard boxes and move on. I wonder now if I am too encumbered by things, too tied down. Is it possible for me to live deliberately and simply even today?

Not so simple?

As I look back on our life as students, I realize that our so-called simple life was really not so simple at times. Nostalgia aside, being frugal and living simply are not entirely the same thing.

Yes, not having a television meant more time for study, reading novels, playing games, and visiting with friends. It made us rich in conversation and rich in opportunities to use our own imaginations and creativity. Ah, the simple life!

But I also remember when we moved from Elkhart to Virginia. Whenever we wanted to treat ourselves to an evening of television at home, my husband would trek over to the seminary audiovisual room, sign out a television and lug it all the way across campus and up two flights of stairs to our apartment, and then figure out a way to get good reception with the rabbit-ear antenna. It was cheap, but it certainly wasn't simple!

As I discovered during those years, sometimes simple living could be complicated. It often required more time—I couldn't just hop into the car whenever I wanted to go somewhere, and because it could be well over an hour between one bus and the next, I might need to wait. Simple living wasn't always convenient and often meant more planning. For example, since I didn't use debit or credit cards, I needed to make sure I would have cash on hand whenever I went for groceries.

Most of all, I came to understand that living simply means more than simply cutting household and personal consumption. That's an important practice, given the impact on the environment, the needs of people around the world, and the lopsided consumption patterns that favor those who already have more than enough. Besides, it's not only cheaper to give up packaged foods in favor of cooking from scratch, but it can also be healthier, better for the environment, more creative, more fun, and just as delicious, if not more so. What's not to like about all of that?

But living simply is about much more. It goes much deeper than our outward, visible practices to our inward disposition. As Richard Foster says, "the Christian discipline of simplicity is an *inward* reality that results in an *outward* life-style. Both the inward and outward aspects of simplicity are essential."[2] An inner simplicity will mean some kind of outward expression. And unless our outward practices are rooted in our inner spiritual life, they may become difficult to sustain, or turn into legalism. So simplicity is not only outward, but inward. Simplicity is not only about letting go of the things of this life; it also means being centered on what really matters.

> **Therefore I tell you, do not worry about your life, what you will eat or what you will drink, or about your body, what you will wear. Is not life more than food, and the body more than clothing? Look at the birds of the air; they neither sow nor reap nor gather into barns, and yet your heavenly Father feeds them. Are you not of more value than they? (Matthew 6:25-26).**

The life of the psalmist was simple not only because he lived close to the land and unencumbered by the consumer culture so characteristic of our time and place. For the psalmist, simplicity also meant singleness of mind and heart: "One thing I asked of the LORD, that will I seek after: to live in the house of the LORD all the days of my life, to behold the beauty of the LORD, and to inquire in his temple."[3]

In his Sermon on the Mount, Jesus tells his followers they cannot serve both God and wealth—they can be faithful to only one master.[4] He tells them not to worry about what they will eat or drink or wear; instead, they are to "strive first for the kingdom of God and his righteousness, and all these things will be given to you as well."[5] Instead of chasing after many different desires and goals, they are to be confident of God's provision and focus on God's kingdom to shape and direct their lives.

One day, when Jesus is at the home of Mary and Martha, Mary sits listening to Jesus while Martha is busy with many

---

2. Richard Foster, *Celebration of Discipline* (San Francisco: Harper & Row, 1978), 69.
3. Psalm 27:4.
4. Matthew 6:24.
5. Matthew 6:33.

tasks. Feeling overburdened by her responsibilities, Martha says, "Lord, do you not care that my sister has left me to do all the work by myself? Tell her then to help me." Surprisingly, Jesus replies, "Martha, Martha, you are worried and distracted by many things; there is need of only one thing. Mary has chosen the better part, which will not be taken away from her." Jesus does care about Martha, but his solution is different from hers. Instead of asking Mary to help, Jesus reminds Martha that of all her many concerns, she needs just one central focus.[6]

Like Martha, we sometimes get busy with many things, overburdened by all the responsibilities that we carry, both real and imagined. We can be just as worried and distracted as Martha appears to be in this story. If I had been in her place, I might have felt rather disappointed and hurt by Jesus' response. But I like to think that Martha was able to receive Jesus' gentle rebuke, that she was able to set aside whatever she was doing to sit and listen to Jesus, that later on Mary and everyone else would pitch in to do whatever needed doing.

Like the psalmist, Mary's one thing was to seek after God. Instead of being distracted by many things, she set her heart on one thing, to listen to her Lord. As Jesus taught in the Sermon on the Mount, Mary was not worried about getting things done, but seeking first God's kingdom in the person of Jesus. As philosopher and theologian Søren Kierkegaard would write later in the nineteenth century, "Purity of heart is to will one thing."[7] That describes Mary, and it describes the kind of simplicity that Jesus wanted also for Martha and for all of us.

How not to do it all

Like Martha, we may act as if we need to manage everything single-handedly, but even the busiest, most efficient person can

---

6. Luke 10:38-42.
7. Søren Kierkegaard, *Purity of Heart Is to Will One Thing*, Douglas V. Steere, tr. (New York: Harper & Brothers Publishers, 1938, 1948).

never do everything there is to do. Having it all and doing it all are merely illusions, for we are limited human beings with limited time and energy. We're not meant to have it all or do it all. We're not meant to rush around and feel irritated when others don't live up to our expectations. Instead, the practice of simplicity can center us inwardly and outwardly.

That means listening to Jesus as Mary did and paying attention to our priorities as Jesus encouraged Martha to do. With this in mind, consider the following four steps:

(1) *Frame.* One of the things that has been helpful for me is to get the big picture. To Martha, Jesus says "only one thing" is needful. In the Sermon on the Mount, he describes it as following God instead of money, seeking first the kingdom of God instead of being anxious. The psalmist describes his one thing as being in the temple, which was his way of seeking after God. So the simple life isn't really about not having a microwave or not owning a smartphone, or any other kind of legalism; instead, the big picture is the simplicity of seeking after God, and it's within that frame that everything else takes place.

(2) *Focus.* Within that frame, I need to focus. There are many ways of seeking after God, many ways of serving in God's kingdom. And in the same way, there are many different versions of living simply. As Albert Hsu writes:

> All of us have different criteria for what we might deem unnecessary. For some, it might be brand-name clothing. For others, it might be electronic and computer equipment. . . . There are no easy answers, or one-size-fits-all approaches to simple living. Simplicity is ultimately a spiritual discipline to be practiced in response to the calling and leading of God.[8]

What he says about material things applies as well to the way we use our time. There too, simplicity is a spiritual discipline

---

8. Albert Y. Hsu, *The Suburban Christian: Finding Spiritual Vitality in the Land of Plenty* (Downers Grove, IVP Books, 2006), 93–94.

that takes careful discernment and will vary from person to person and at different stages of life.

One year, I kept a list of all the things I said no to: invitations to join a committee, speaking engagements, social gatherings, a new job opportunity, donation requests, other responsibilities or activities. I appreciated being asked, and each thing was good and worthwhile, but they were also too much. Some things conflicted with other commitments. So I couldn't attend a fundraiser banquet since I was out of town visiting family that same weekend. Some things required more than I could give. I was already stretched between family and home life, full-time pastoral ministry, and writing. "Your plate is full," one of my sisters said to me. "You need a platter!"

But if I turned my plate into a platter, I'd likely need a bigger and bigger platter, too. What I really needed to do was focus. What's essential and what's not? What needs my attention, and what do I need to set aside? Every so often, I would look at my list of nos and reassure myself. All these things had gone well without me; the funds had been raised, someone else was serving on the committee, someone else had taken on the new board position. Saying no to these things had left me free to say yes in other areas. I didn't need to do it all.

> In the Sermon on the Mount, Jesus says, "Let your word be 'Yes, Yes' or 'No, No'; anything more than this comes from the evil one" (Matthew 5:37). With these words, Jesus addresses the ancient practice of swearing as a guarantee of truthfulness; instead of relying on such oaths, Jesus teaches his followers to be truthful at all times. His words also apply to keeping our commitments. If I say yes to something, then I really need to follow through and do it. If my plate is already full, I don't need to pretend I can take on more. I can simply let my no be no.

(3) *Fill.* I've been reading lately about the downside of multitasking, how trying to do several things at once can actually be less productive than focusing on one thing at time, how switching from task to task can actually cost time and money due to

the loss of concentration in between. When it comes to driving and cell phones, multitasking can even be dangerous, so where I live, drivers must use hands-free cell phones or face a fine for using a cell phone while driving.

And yet there are times when multitasking seems entirely appropriate. I like to listen to the news while I wash dishes, to do the crossword puzzle while I'm watching television. If you've ever gone grocery shopping with a five-year-old, multitasking is a necessary skill. Parenting is multitasking. Driving is multitasking. Even without the distraction of a cell phone, just think about monitoring your speed while staying in your lane while seeing the traffic light turn yellow and deciding whether to stop or keep going, being aware of the teenagers on the corner about to step out into the street.

Multitasking is not necessarily bad, but the trick is to know when it's appropriate and when it's not. There's nothing wrong with doing my household filing or reading a book while I'm waiting on hold for the telephone company. But if I'm on the phone with a friend who's just returned from her cousin's funeral, it's time to set other things aside. Simplicity means that I don't need to be multitasking every moment. Instead, I can slow down to pay attention to one thing at a time.

(4) *Forever*. As I frame, focus, and fill my time, I also find it helpful to think in terms of eternity. What are the tasks that are just for the moment, and which ones will have a lasting impact? Which tasks contribute to forming good relationships with God and with other people? Which tasks won't matter a week from now, a year from now? What seems most immediate may not actually be the most important. The Forever Principle helps me to simplify by clarifying my priorities.

Sacred pause: simplify

The practice of simplicity involves both our inner life and our outer life, both our use of things and our use of time. Each of the following exercises focuses on just one of these areas, but each area is related to all the others. For example, as we become more centered on God inwardly, we may also find ourselves becoming less distracted in our outward life. Simplifying our possessions can help to simplify the way we use our time, since having fewer things means having fewer things to take care of. As we become more deliberate about our use of time, we may have more time for prayer and centering on God. So when we simplify in one area, we may find ourselves simplifying in other areas as well.

- *Inner life.* Jesus says to Martha, "only one thing is needful." Reflect on your own spiritual life. What is the one thing that is needful for you?

- *Outer life.* As you go about your daily tasks, be calm and focused. Let your yes be yes, and your no be no. As difficulties arise, turn them over to God. Let go of any anxieties.

- *Possessions.* Simplify your possessions by giving away things that you don't need. If you haven't worn something in your closet for the last two years, send it off to a good home. If you have more dishes or linens than you need, give them to someone else who can use them.

- *Time.* Consider a specific time frame in the coming week—an hour, an afternoon, a day. Where do you need to focus? How will you fill the time? By multitasking or attending to one thing at a time? What is important in terms of forever?

18

Ending Well

The LORD is my strength and my shield; in him my heart trusts;
so I am helped, and my heart exults,
and with my song I give thanks to him.
Psalm 28:7

The summer before I started high school, a friend invited me to take part in a week of church youth camp. I think of that as my first retreat in a beautiful setting along the water; fresh air; archery, crafts, and other fun activities during the day; evening devotionals around the campfire; whispering and giggling into the night with the other girls in my cabin. When the week was over, we girls sat together on the ferry ride back home and relived our camp experience with stories, laughter, and tears. By the time we got off the boat, we were all crying so hard that my parents could hear us even before they saw us. "Why were you all crying?" my mother asked.

I couldn't answer her then. I had had such a good time away; I was glad to be home; I would see my friends again soon, so there was really no reason for tears. I didn't know why I was crying any more than she did. But looking back now, I think my tears were part of the intensity of the whole experience. It was the first time I had been away from my family for a whole week, the first time bonding with a group of girls outside of family or school, the first time encountering God in a setting other than church. It had been an intense and immensely satisfying time away from my usual life, and my tears were a welcome relief.

I no longer remember how the leaders ended that week of youth camp, but I know now that the way a retreat ends can be just as important as the beginning and middle. Careful planning right to the end can help tie together the different parts of a retreat, sum up the experience in a meaningful way, and bring the time to completion before saying goodbye and moving on. As retreat leader Shirley R. Harman recommends, "Whether the retreat lasts one day or two weeks, plan a significant time and activity to conclude the group experience. It can be a time of affirmation, of summary, of praise, of dedication, of celebration, of decision—whatever response seems most appropriate to the purpose and outcome of the retreat."[1]

Journal Prompt

Describe a time when you were moved to tears. The birth of your child? The death of a parent? A winning goal by your favorite team? A tragic movie? How would you explain your tears? What beginning or ending did they represent for you?

As you near the end of this book, I hope you will also end well. Whether you've completed this book as a daily retreat in three weeks, or in a lot more or a lot less time, whether or not you've skipped sections or skipped around, this is a good time to consider how far you've come to bring this stage to completion and then carry on. Using Harman's list, consider the following options. Again, the point is not necessarily to try everything, or even to do anything exactly as described, but to spark your own imagination as the Spirit moves you. What might be the most appropriate ending for you at this point?

Affirmation. Write a statement of affirmation, and say it out loud to yourself in a mirror, or if that sounds too crazy to you, then just sit in a comfortable chair and close your eyes. Here's my affirmation statement: "Taking sacred pauses has been good for me. I have connected with God in new ways, and I look

1. Shirley R. Harman, *Retreat Planning Made Easy* (Minneapolis: Augsburg Publishing House, 1985), 25.

forward to keeping connected." What affirmations can you make about your experience?

Summary. As you look back on your spiritual practice, what one word would you choose to describe your experience? Unexpected, different, experimental, curious, confusing, fitting, mysterious, difficult, fleeting, forgettable, transforming, unsettling, peaceful, informative, educational, nurturing, constraining, liberating, creative? Use a dictionary or a thesaurus if you need help in finding just the right word. What have you learned about yourself? About God? Read through all of your journal entries, and make a new entry that sums up your experience.

> Psalm 139 begins with the assurance of God's presence: "O LORD, you have searched me and known me. You know when I sit down and when I rise up" (vv. 1-2). The psalm continues to describe God's presence everywhere, anywhere, and at all times. Now we come full circle: "How weighty to me are your thoughts, O God! How vast is the sum of them! I try to count them—they are more than the sand; I come to the end—I am still with you" (vv. 17-18).

Praise. Read aloud a psalm of praise such as Psalm 33 or Psalm 117. Add a hand clap at the end of each line, or sing a song, light candles, or choose some other act of praise that is meaningful to you. Think over your experience, and write your own psalm of praise. Be specific. How has God led you? How has God been revealed to you? Psalm 136 repeats "his steadfast love endures forever." What refrain might express your feelings of praise?

Dedication. Think back to the everyday icon that you chose in chapter 1. Has it helped to remind you to pause? (Re)dedicate it for this purpose if you so choose. Is God calling you to dedicate yourself in some way—to morning prayer, to give a consistent percentage of your income to God's work, to some other kind of spiritual practice?

Celebration. Last Friday, I celebrated the end of the week by sneaking one of the last few Nanaimo bars out of the freezer and savoring it slowly with a cup of hot tea. Consider what kind of food or activity might help you celebrate this stage of your life and spiritual practice. Starting a new page in your journal? Going for a long walk? Something else?

Decision. As we pay attention to our inner life, we may also gain clarity about our identity, purpose, and next steps in our outward life. Like the man who returns from retreat determined to make some changes in his work life. Or a young person who returns from summer camp eager to go on to Bible college. As you have spent time in silence, prayer, and attending to God in other ways, have you also come to any decisions about your life?

Giving thanks. This is my own addition to Harman's list. As you think back over your experience of weaving spiritual practices into your daily life, give thanks for God's leading. Reread each of your journal entries and add the refrain from Psalm 103 after each: "Bless the Lord!" Write your own gratitude list. When talk show host Oprah Winfrey introduced the gratitude journal to her viewers, one woman wrote: 1. I am grateful to have my God in my life. 2. I am grateful for the little moments of pure silence during the day. 3. Books. 4. Poetry. 5. I am profoundly grateful for the view outside my window. Another entry listed: Love. Life. Health. My children. My dog. When you pause to consider your life, what makes you thankful?

However you choose to end your time, be deliberate and make it meaningful for you. Think of it as another pause in the action. This is a time to give thanks, to recognize where you are, to regroup before moving on. Take time for this now.

Afterword

Going Deeper

Deep calls to deep at the thunder of your cataracts
all your waves and your billows have gone over me.
By day the LORD commands his steadfast love,
and at night his song is with me,
a prayer to the God of my life.
Psalm 42:7-8

As I was researching and writing this book, I came across this paragraph that almost made me quit:

> Spiritual disciplines call us away from a bloated faith that doesn't let us squeeze the Savior into our schedules. They call us away from an anorexic faith in which we fail to absorb sufficient nutrients for spiritual health.
>
> They call us away from a bulimic faith that compels us to binge on Christian beliefs on Sunday morning but to purge them up on Monday morning. A regular diet of spiritual disciplines gives us the health we need for communion with God, the stamina we need to advance his kingdom, and the strength we need to battle the world, the flesh and the devil.[1]

At once I had to say "Amen!" What a challenge, and what a clear case for spiritual disciplines! And yet my heart also sank as I thought about my attempts to weave spiritual practices into my day. Am I simply trying to squeeze the Savior into my

1. Christian George, *Sacred Travels: Recovering the Ancient Practice of Pilgrimage* (Downers Grove: IVP Press, 2006), 15.

own schedule? Am I lacking in sufficient nutrients for spiritual health?

I really didn't need these questions to remind me that I still have a long way to go. I know how much I long for a deeper, more spacious, and more mature life in the Spirit, how laughable really that I should be trying to write a book on spiritual discipline. But I take heart from these words of Thomas Merton: "We do not want to be beginners. But let us be convinced of the fact that we will never be anything else but beginners."[2] What he says about prayer applies more generally to the spiritual life too. In the deep things of the Spirit, we are all beginners and always will be, whoever and wherever we may be.

Just as evangelism has sometimes been described as one beggar telling another beggar where there is bread, that applies here too. When it comes to spiritual practice, we are all like beggars telling other beggars where there is bread to nourish our souls. In that sense, I am both beginner and beggar, looking for a place to begin and longing for more.

There is so much more to explore in Scripture, prayer, fasting, paying attention, and the other spiritual practices in this book. Beyond these personal exercises, there are also many more shared disciplines: spiritual friendship, spiritual direction,

> *Journal Prompt*
>
> **Think of a time when you felt like quitting something, giving up on a particular project, going back on a promise, breaking a commitment. Did you persevere? Why or why not? How was God part of your decision making?**

> **Nevertheless I am continually with you;**
> **you hold my right hand.**
> **You guide me with your counsel, and afterward you will receive me with honor.**
> **Whom have I in heaven but you? And there is nothing on earth that I desire other than you.**
> **My flesh and my heart may fail, but God is the strength of my heart and my portion forever (Psalm 73:23-26).**

---

2. Thomas Merton, Excerpts from *Contemplative Prayer*, in Richard J. Foster and James Bryan Smith, eds., *Devotional Classics* (Harper: San Francisco, 1993), 64.

hospitality, community, corporate confession, corporate worship, corporate prayer. Far from being comprehensive, this book is just one way of thinking about spiritual practice, and there are many, many more avenues to explore.

As you continue from here, you may wish to revisit some of your favorite spiritual practices, or go over days that you somehow missed. Ongoing spiritual practice can be a way of life. Not because there is some rule that says you have to, not because the spiritual practices in themselves will change you, but because God is at work in and through the different spiritual practices, and in and through you.

Our steps are made firm by the LORD,
when he delights in our way;
though we stumble, we shall not fall headlong,
for the LORD holds us by the hand.
Psalm 37:23-24

Recommended Resources

Barton, Ruth Haley. *Sacred Rhythms: Arranging Our Lives for Spiritual Transformation*. Downers Grove: IVP Books, 2006. An engaging exploration of spiritual practice. I especially appreciate the last chapter on developing your own personal rhythm.

Boers, Arthur Paul. *The Way Is Made by Walking: A Pilgrimage Along the Camino de Santiago*. Downers Grove: IVP Books, 2007. A story of pilgrimage—part personal experience, part theological reflection.

Calhoun, Adele Ahlberg. *Spiritual Disciplines Handbook: Practices that Transform Us*. Downers Grove: IVP Books, 2005. A handbook of personal and corporate spiritual practices.

Foster, Richard J. *Celebration of Discipline: The Path to Spiritual Growth*. San Francisco: Harper & Row, 1978. A classic introduction to spiritual discipline.

Foster, Richard J. and Gayle D. Beebe. *Longing for God: Seven Paths of Christian Devotion*. Downers Grove: IVP Books, 2009. An introduction to spiritual writers throughout history.

Hawkins, Pamela C. *Behold! Cultivating Attentiveness in the Season of Advent*. Nashville: Upper Room Books, 2011. A seasonal resource, for use alone or with a small group.

Hess, Valerie E. *Spiritual Disciplines Devotional: A Year of Readings*. Downers Grove: IVP Books, 2007. An introduction to spiritual disciplines, with daily readings.

Houser, Gordon. *Present Tense: a Mennonite Spirituality.* Telford, PA: Cascadia Publishing, 2011.
Practice, Patience, Peace, Politics, Play, Prayer, Perfection, Presence.

Hsu, Albert Y. *The Suburban Christian: Finding Spiritual Vitality in the Land of Plenty.* Downers Grove: IVP Books, 2006.
Historical, social, and theological reflection on suburban life and Christian spirituality.

Johnson, Jan. *Spiritual Disciplines Companion: Bible Studies and Practices to Transform Your Soul.* Downers Grove: IVP Books, 2009.
Spiritual practices linked with Bible studies from both Old and New Testaments.

Klimoski, Victor J., ed. *Illuminating Ministry: A Journal.* Collegeville, MN: Liturgical Press, 2010.
A beautiful journal that includes images from *The Saint John's Bible* and directed reflections on hospitality, community, and other themes.

Lanzetta, Beverly. *40-Day Journey Series.* Minneapolis: Augsburg Books, 2007.
A series featuring the poet Gerard Manley Hopkins, writer Madeleine L'Engle, and other men and women whose writings serve as a guide for reflection and prayer.

Leng, Felicity (compiler). *Invincible Spirits: A Thousand Years of Women's Spiritual Writings.* Grand Rapids: Eerdmans, 2007.
From St. Teresa of Avila to Simone Weil, from Julian of Norwich to Dorothy Sayers, and many more.

Silf, Margaret. *Going on Retreat: A Beginner's Guide to the Christian Retreat Experience.* Chicago: Loyola Press, 2002.
An overview of Christian retreat, including the daily-life retreat.

Silf, Margaret. *Inner Compass: An Invitation to Ignatian Spirituality.* Chicago: Loyola Press, 1999.

A helpful introduction to Ignatian spirituality in contemporary language, with personal examples, suggestions for prayer and reflection.

Taylor, Barbara Brown. *An Altar in the World: A Geography of Faith*. New York: HarperOne, 2009.

The Practice of Waking Up to God, The Practice of Getting Lost, The Practice of Feeling Pain, and other ways of encountering God.

Acknowledgments

Thank you to family, church members, colleagues, friends, students, and even passing acquaintances who have made comments and shared your personal stories with me. You may not have realized how much your words and experiences would stay with me, and I didn't know at the time that they would one day become part of this book. I am grateful to God for weaving you into my life.

To Byron Rempel-Burkholder and Amy Gingerich of Herald Press, thank you for your notes, questions, thoughtful responses, and collaborative approach. To Arthur Boers, I appreciate your clarity, wisdom, and generosity. Your foreword is a gift.

Thank you to Emmanuel Mennonite Church for your love and support. From the beginning, your call to me as pastor has included room for my writing both for and beyond the church. I live out that calling with great care and joy with all of you.

I would also like to acknowledge *Mennonite World Review*, which first published an early version of the portion on reading Scripture, and *Christian Living*, which first published the portion on simple living.

As always, I am grateful for my husband, Gary, for your constant love and encouragement. Thank you for everything.

> *I will bless the Lord at all times;*
> *his praise shall continually be in my mouth.*
> *Psalm 34:1*

The Author

April Yamasaki is lead pastor of Emmanuel Mennonite Church in Abbotsford, British Columbia. She has published numerous articles and several books, including *Remember Lot's Wife and Other Unnamed Women of the Bible* (FaithQuest) and *Making Disciples: A Manual for Baptism and Church Membership* (Faith & Life Press). She has a bachelor of arts degree from the University of British Columbia, a master's degree in Christian studies from Regent College, Vancouver, BC, and enjoyed seminary life along with her husband at Anabaptist Mennonite  Biblical Seminary in Elkhart, Indiana, and Union Presbyterian Seminary in Richmond, Virginia.

April has taught college-level courses in Bible and English, adult enrichment courses on prayer and journaling, and seminars and retreats on Christian living.

A third-generation Canadian of Chinese descent, she was born and raised in Vancouver, BC. April lives in Abbotsford with her husband, Gary, who teaches biblical studies at Columbia Bible College.

Visit her website at www.aprilyamasaki.com.